Musings

On Development Impulse

Arun Sapre

ISBN 979-8-89610-955-6

Contents

Preface 7

1. Development – Thinking Beyond Survival 9
2. Role of Science in Developing Technology 14
3. Technology in Development 20
4. Of Spin-offs and Take-offs 25
5. Appetizer for Technology 30
6. Big is Inevitable 34
7. Catalysing Sustainable Urbanisation 39
8. Consequences of Competition 44
9. Progress Breeded Destruction 49
10. Professions and Sensitivity 54
11. Motivating Leadership 59
12. Championing Simplicity 64
13. Sustaining an Idea or a Mission 69

14.	Platitudes vs Performance	73
15.	Looking to Deliver Results	78
16.	Priming Body and Mind	83
17.	Finding Traction to Perform Better	88
18.	Keep Innovating for Progress	93
19.	Education: Preparing Minds for Innovations	97
20.	Motivation for Innovation – Raising Pedestal	101
21.	Impulse for Creativity	106
22.	Shield of Afterthoughts	111
23.	Skill, Knowledge and Action	116
24.	Understanding Knowledge	121
25.	Case of Tacit Knowledge	126
26.	Survival vs Knowledge Seeking	131
27.	Crisis of Overdose	136
28.	Other Side of Development	141
29.	Look at the Other Side	146
30.	Contrasts Coexist	150
31.	Victim of Own Success	155
32.	Toppers to Tail-enders	160
33.	Thinking – A Nature's Gift	165
34.	Commercialisation of Human Senses	170

35. Rarity of Long Term Thinking 175

36. Sustainable Thinking 180

37. Wasting Time 185

38. Unease of Side Effects 190

39. Maturity, Wisdom and Harmony with Nature 195

40. Education for all, a misnomer? 200

41. Building Character 205

About the Book *211*

About the author *213*

Synopsis *215*

Preface

My earlier books "Musings : On Human Nature" and "Musings : On Social Life" dealt with some topics related to human nature and behaviour in social context. These are complex subjects and much has been written, researched and articulated in different forms of literary, philosophical and artistic presentations. Human mind and behaviour is not fully understood. The realities still remain elusive and human efforts to understand these continue. The complexity is mind boggling and provides scope for diverse views, assessments, interpretations as also for further studies and research in changing situations and contexts. This book is one such attempt.

The present book "Musings: On Development Impulse" is a compilation of articles on topics related to a broader theme of development and progress as an evolutionary process of change in living conditions. These are independent articles written at different times. These are personal views on varied topics which came to mind and prompted to put in article format. Providing unbiased, positive, honest and broader views is the intent. Yearning for development, influence of knowledge build-up, technological contribution, socio-economic context, attitudinal changes and impact of combined efforts is attempted to understand. My science background and professional experience has prompted me to gauge the natural causation in the development process. The topics are generic and linked to common observations and diverse perceptions. The articles give personal views and try to convey perceived realities. Opinions are formed based on personal experiences, diverse readings and wide interactions.

I express my sincere thanks to Mr. Nitin Gadre and Mr. Prakash Joshi for reading the articles and giving frank opinions. They inspired me to put the articles in public domain. My sincere thanks to Mrs. Seema Ranalkar for creative and appropriate cover page design. My sincere thanks to the Notion Press Team for professional help in bringing out this third book "Musings : On Development Impulse".

Arun Sapre

Development – Thinking Beyond Survival

Everyone born wants to survive. Only when the survival is assured, one tries to look beyond for development or progress. Early childhood, family and social background, education, physical assets, exposure to real life situations, surrounding conditions and many other influencing factors contribute to mental make-up of any individual. Motivations and objectives emerge from this complex process. Why a person acts in a particular manner could be reasonably explained by looking at his/her situation and the mind-set evolved over the preceding life span. To be cautious or aggressive or ambitious or indifferent, or to play safe or to take a middle path etc. are the approaches one gets into based on the mind-set evolved over a period of time. Likes and dislikes, fascinations, fears, attachments, commitment, devotion etc. are normally built up during the childhood. Unless counteracted/overwhelmed by larger forces for a change, these characteristics remain entrenched throughout the life span. In majority of the cases, motivations and objectives are set during the childhood and formative years. Modest goals and playing safe is the normal approach.

Primary focus for any individual is survival. If the very survival is under challenge, one cannot think of anything else. First thing first is the approach and rightly so. Poverty stricken population keeps struggling for survival and any sermons regarding bigger ambitions of development would not deter them from looking beyond that objective. To bring them out of this mind-set, only a larger societal action that provides a safety net, ensuring survival, and credible opportunities would be needed. Most of the developing countries find this quite difficult and continue to struggle for development. Creating income opportunities to all is a crucial factor to ensure survival of all and look beyond. The task is quite challenging and everyone is struggling for a right path.

When survival is reasonably assured, an individual is likely to think more of progress and new ideas to achieve certain ambitions. Social security programmes in some developed countries such as food subsidies, unemployment allowances and employment guarantee programmes are some of the safety nets created to assure survival income. Those taking advantages of these schemes are expected and encouraged to search for regular jobs or self-employment. It is a facilitating mechanism to stabilise in a survival state and step into the growth mode. In the process, personal motivation, merit, skill, capacity and expectations are not undermined and, in fact, are tested for gauging worth of the individual to stand on own feet. It is an opportunity to move from survival to growth.

Depending upon the personal ambition and capacity, one can shift from personal benefits to family benefits to societal benefits. With personal stability one thinks of welfare of the family members. If the growth achieved goes beyond these requirements, people do think of extended family and even the community at large. That is where one observes charitable actions of individuals in the form of help to the needy and setting up of charitable institutions for wider operations. The strength of such network of institutions in the society indicates the level of social security as a public action.

Stronger the network, greater is the chance to think beyond survival and to develop. Supplemented by the government schemes, this process of development and value creation could get momentum.

Although development is achieved through motivation and drive, the material benefits that it may provide may not get the individual carried away to a wrong path. If the means cross the needs, sane individual starts thinking about charitable actions or creative endeavours. There are many outstanding examples of charity and creative works by rich individuals those have left a permanent mark on the society at large. Museums, hospitals, educational institutions, facilities for handicapped, cultural facilities, developmental organisations etc. are revealing examples of social actions by haves for have-nots. A secured individual with creative and original thinking is likely to do something path-breaking. Such individuals would have sensitivity and feeling for common good and attachment to nature and its bounties. They do recognise the importance of survival of all, the nature's preference for diversity and need of polyculture for sustainability. They use their means to work for the society and the nature which for them is more valuable than personal greed.

For accelerating development, it is necessary to rejuvenate the have-nots to perform. By bringing them out of the survival trap it is possible to motivate them to utilise their hidden potential. Rekindling the flame in them to self-realise their potential is the most reliable path for development. A feeling of helplessness has to be replaced by a feeling of confidence. There are proven ways to achieve this. These confidence building measures include extensive decentralisation of social actions for downstream involvement, support to entrepreneurship and focus on employment generation. The sense of belonging in the process and the resultant willingness to perform better could provide the best results. A wider participation and grass-root level action is crucial for achieving faster results.

Any development that ignores nature's rules, natural resources and bio-diversity is detrimental in the long run. Nurturing and conserving the nature need to be the basis of development. This should cover all natural habitats, their interdependence, preservation of genetic pool, conservation of natural resources and emphasis on renewable resources. Sustainable development has to be the ultimate objective. Understanding the nature, limitations on development, long term impact of human actions and sensitivity towards all species need to be the guiding principles for development. Those who have tried to understand these principles have been instrumental in creating localised successful working models in all parts of the world. These success stories are outcomes of creative and dedicated efforts by individuals and institutions. There is always a pleasure in creativity and positive contribution. Individuals do have fascination for creative action than placid routines. If it is of benefit to the people and the nature, it needs to be encouraged. That is the effective form of social action. That is how one could think beyond survival and inspire all to develop, and that too in a creative fashion, and in harmony with nature.

Development has relative connotation. Progress, enrichment, amelioration, positive change, satisfying needs, happiness etc are various facets of development. Moving in that direction is the attempt. It is the united action, always facing contradictions and dilemmas. Yet the thinking is forward looking and movement is positive. Come out of the cocoon, give up the frozen condition, don't be inert, tread the uncharted path, take risk, be adventurous, show gusto, bravo etc are the type of remarks those inspire and give outlet to the hidden passion in the individual. The human spirit cultivates learning, exploration and creation. To understand things around, pick up what is useful and attractive, pass on new knowledge and tools to others and make the living better is all that is being attempted. Success or failure do not stop the attempt. Combined effect of all these efforts is a forward movement. The change is visible and positive. Development goes on in spite of challenge to survival.

Role of Science in Developing Technology

Technologies have brought about many transformations during the past couple of centuries. Significant changes have been observed in the economic activities, social reforms, urbanization and overall quality of life. Progress in technology continues unabated. However, the ideas for technologies come from work in basic sciences. At the same time, new technologies facilitate new research in the basic sciences. So both are showing complementary and interdependent development.

Basic Sciences

The term science got evolved in early Nineteenth Century. Before that it was known as natural philosophy. In that sense science is a study of nature or can also be called as language to explain nature. In spite of common language of communication, each scientific discipline has its own vocabulary. So there are words with special meanings used in different subjects such as physical, chemical, mathematical and biological sciences, engineering etc. With growth of science and technology this vocabulary is also growing,

In a way, basic sciences is a source of new ideas, well placed to understand the unknowns of nature. Science finds new principles and new insights about the nature. This cognitive process is the method of science that helps further understanding of nature. These scientific principles also help in suggesting new ideas for development of tools and technologies of benefit in our daily life and in various economic activities. For example, mathematics has provided algorithms for computers, chemistry has provided medicines to health service, physics has provided inputs to communication technology, biology has provided inputs to vaccines etc. Essentially science is a source of new ideas for technology development and application.

Technologies

Technology is called as science in action as the motive is to develop useful knowledge and useful technologies beneficial in various human activities. In fact, development of useful knowledge is the main motive/objective in scientific research. This objective is specifically mentioned while setting up American Philosophical Society by Benjamin Franklin. The important strength of technology is in value creation. Any natural resource gets its value due to technology. So even a waste becomes a resource with the help of technology. This strength of technology is now well established and there is a clear trend in developing new technologies to put everything to use.

Technology is also creating new applications of benefit to the people. The last century has seen technology after technology getting developed and changing economic and social structure. One can mention, as examples, electricity, IC engine, atomic energy, space technology, chemicals, polymers, electronics, computers, biotechnology etc. which have completely changed the life. Technologies have not only met the necessities but have also created new necessities. Mobile telephone is the latest example of this kind. In fact, presently, it has become the biggest new necessity of everyone.

Looking at the developments in science and technology one can consider them as a useful knowledge. Putting it to use needs efforts to understand it clearly. It is not just information that can be called knowledge but it is more often the ability and skill to decipher information. One can easily understand the interdependence of information and knowledge. Knowledge is also linked to creation of new skills, new applications and new avenues for development. Knowledge could be misused for dangerous activities. Knowledge is also some kind of illusion as there are many unknowns which may prop up by its use. Unknown effects like pollution, degeneration of biodiversity, climate change, new viruses etc. are examples which suggest caution in use of new technology or knowledge.

Information is normally codified or explicit knowledge that is available in public domain and freely available. However, there is also uncodified knowledge which is individual centred. One can call it insight or common sense of individual, varying with individual and cannot be fully gauged. This is the tacit knowledge that stays with the individual. Transferring this tacit knowledge is difficult. These are deeper understandings or nuances of the individual developed with personal experiences and personal ability. It is also linked with judgmental insight or hunch of the individual as is commonly known. Ultimately, it is the tacit knowledge that differentiates individual from individual.

Innovation:

Pursuit of knowledge is for understanding the nature. This leads to discoveries or revelations of natural phenomena. This understanding of nature does not stop with discovery. The next step is to utilize discovery to do something new. This inventiveness is a result of the desire to utilize new knowledge for benefit of the people. Methods of use of scientific discoveries drives the inventiveness and development of technology. However, one cannot stop with invention alone. To make use of this invention requires consideration of other related factors such as linkages with needs, operationalization and economic basis to make use of these inventions. This step is where invention becomes innovation by which commercialization becomes possible.

Inventions are basically iterative. They lead to more inventions. Naturally, innovations keep getting strength and increasingly intrusive. So new innovations are more powerful, more useful, more efficient and even more destructive. Although Necessities are considered as mother of inventions, the inventions also have the potential to create new necessities. The passage of the discovery to invention to innovation experiences many valleys of death. The successful innovations crossing these valleys of death succeed in commercialization.

In the innovation chain, technology is only one parameter. The other parameters which have to be taken care of include acceptance of technology by users, economic feasibility, convenience of use and tangible benefits to be accrued. This economic angle brings in the role of finance, risk management and market demand. That is where the role of venture funds, angel finance, crowd funding, marketing and management comes in. The process of innovation also needs consideration of issues related to Intellectual Property Rights (IPR), environmental effects and sustainability of the products. So innovation is a multifaceted process of change. Strong technological background, existence of related infrastructure, research capabilities and strength in selected product lines generally create monopolies and brands. This is a common experience of the past couple of centuries.

Big Science:

The earlier discoveries up to eighteenth century were mostly termed as natural philosophy. These activities were individual based and most of the discoveries have remained in the name of the concerned individuals. The word science for these activities got introduced in early nineteenth century. The basic science mostly covered physics, chemistry, biology and mathematics. However, as the science built up during nineteenth and twentieth centuries, many new sub-disciplines and specializations came into existence. For example, physics became physical sciences which include solid state physics, electronics, materials science, astrophysics, theoretical physics and so on. The scientific activities since latter part of twentieth century are known more as multi-disciplinary science or big science or team science.

The technologies getting generated find inputs from variety of industries and variety of sectors. There exists inter-industry technology flow. So sectors like bio-technology, vacuum technology, automobiles, aeronautics, computers, satellites, medical devices/ implants, pharmaceuticals etc. need inputs from many disciplines. Even the research activities require big experimental set-ups and inputs of big systems. All these become a team activity. This team needs large number of domain experts to take care of individual sections of the system. So activities like space programme or atomic energy or even industrial research, with applications of variety of technologies, need wide range of domain expertise.

Although the big science need many enabling tools and complementary inputs they cannot fully substitute the domain scientific expertise required for the broader objective of the activity. This is where the basic science plays a big role of setting the broader objectives of the mission. Basic sciences are primarily the source of new ideas for new engineering applications. So, Astrophysics may provide the basic parameters for the desired exploration of the cosmos and the engineering will be able to design the systems like variety of large telescopes for these experiments. Similarly, particle physicist may provide specifications to engineers to design big particle accelerators. The basic science have to set the objectives. It also must be accepted that new technologies add to new information that lead to new discoveries. The process goes on, adding to the knowledge pool.

Technology in Development

If science is a study of nature, all that exists around us, its pursuit is a noble and enduring cause. It is a language to describe nature, a cumulative built-up of knowledge about nature. There are many unknowns and what we know is also questionable in the sense that it may undergo changes as we progress. Science leads to technology. Without science there can be no technology. The idea is to use science for benefits of the people. Technology is science in action, a tool to accrue benefits. It consists of both hardware and information, and has economic value. Technology is an outcome of innovation process with a passage from idea to invention to product to commercialization. The developed technology needs to stand the test of utility and economic viability. Primary basis is the scientific principle that generates idea followed by engineering of the product to make it useful. Technology needs to be packaged for delivery to potential users. Innovations help to improve technologies as a continuing activity leading to progress in manufacturing and services.

Development is linked to adding value to our resources, reach out to wider market, generate employment and build economic activity in a competitive environment. It also aims at upgrading agriculture, productive assets, infrastructure and services. Technological innovation plays a crucial role in development.

Facilitating technology transfer and assimilation is a much desired strategy in any economy. Promoting basic research, support to technology generation, technology demonstration and backing its commercialization are important initiatives which need to be inbuilt in this strategy. It is a process that expects the technology to stand on its own strength and merit. Technology transfer is desirable and yet a difficult task as there are many unknowns. It is worth trying to understand these unknowns and options to tackle them.

The influencing factors include individual, social, political, economic, aspirational and environmental constraints in taking innovative technologies to the potential end-users. Every individual has his/her own ways to make choices. Selection of career, profession, job, business, clothing, food, friends and so on are all personal choices difficult to predict or explain. What business and which technology to be chosen is also an individual choice. Outside influence may have a role, but limited one. Social constraints on individual choices are generally connected to family background, business preferences, location constraints, risks involved etc. For example, chemical industry cannot be set up in thickly populated areas, meat processing may not be an acceptable business to vegetarians, mining business is possible in remote and isolated areas, setting up winery may not be possible for all and so on. Polluting technologies could find resistance on socio-political considerations. Environmental issues are becoming crucial and choices of environmentally sound technologies are finding preferences. Technologies providing low return on investment, high volume - low value operations and those experiencing fast obsolescence may find low demand. Economic justification for a venture is the ultimate criteria. Persons with high aspirations and entrepreneurial urge may opt for risky and high-end technology options. These are high-tech ventures with high risk and high return characteristics. So, well considered choice of technologies is a complex process, full of uncertainties and beset with risk of failure.

There are other inherent limits on technology transfer. For example, Intellectual Property issues have come into prominence. Patented processes and know-how licensing have to be looked into while acquiring identified new technology. The legal steps involved need to be understood and gone through. Entrepreneurs not experienced in these issues may feel it as a major hurdle, besides the risk in the working of the technology itself. Big corporates like IBM do a sizeable business by acquiring and pooling patented technologies. Innovative technologies being incubated for start-ups are full of risks in doing business. There are many failures, but the spirit behind is entrepreneurial passion to give it a try. There are quite a few success stories, inspiring many young minds to try their ideas and venture into technology driven businesses. HP, Apple, Microsoft, Google and Amazon are star examples of successful ventures of young entrepreneurs.

Culture of risk taking is central to start-ups. Big players are averse to taking risks with completely new ideas which are suggesting irrelevance of their established practices. They resist change, play safe and eventually perish. Advent of personal computing was the handiwork of freshers that made main-frame computers irrelevant in a short time. Those who failed to adjust to the new reality perished. Disruptive technologies have brought in many changes in communications, textiles, energy, transportation etc. Fresh minds with ideas and entrepreneurial zeal are ready to take risks. Being starters, they have nothing to lose at the beginning and if the idea is sound may attract venture funding to share the risk. Readiness to take risks, passion, frugal overheads and voluntary contributions drive the start-ups. It is also the unique acceptance of disruptive technologies in the existing sectors. Success stories across the sectors indicate this reality.

Recognition of failures due to not accepting new business realities such as technology obsolescence, outdated skill levels, changing consumer choices and improved business practices is a starting point to find a passage towards success. Not trying to gauge the realities and improve upon leads to nothing. At the same time, those who don't participate in the race have no chance of success. Underdogs to heroes are stories often cited. Apple, Microsoft, Google, Amazon etc are success stories scripted by individuals who started from nothing, except an idea. Strange and unknown parameters must have worked in the success stories. These unknowns are difficult to evaluate. But one thing is certain that they did try something new. Keeping with trying new idea provides a glimmer of hope. Not trying provides no hope at all, only staring failure.

The most established and accepted method of technology generation is to invest in research and development as a policy. Such strategic positions are taken at industry as well as government levels. Variety of laboratories and their networks form the organised infrastructure to support innovations in technologies. These are structured activities with clear goals, particularly at industry level, as a business model. Pharma, auto, electronics, power, defence, space etc are some of the sectors which invest big in R&D as a business strategy. To innovate is their goal. In a way, technology development and innovation is an organised activity, particularly in the developed countries, to remain developed. Governments invest in R&D as national policy to boost development through innovations. Emerging sectors are particularly promoted and new frontiers of knowledge are explored as a policy. Investment targets for R&D and research manpower are set consciously. Going on fast track to innovate and exploit the competitive advantage is in mind. Such forward looking policies depict the maturity of thinking in the community and forms the driving force for the leadership to act in that direction. To innovate and develop is the mission worth pursuing.

Of Spin-offs and Take-offs

Scientific discoveries provide the platform for technological innovations and subsequent commercial utilisation. This pattern is well understood in the present organised economic activities driven by progress in science and technology. However, the pattern existed in somewhat lose form even before the advent of modern science and innovative technologies. Many of the present day industrial activities are the spin-offs of discoveries made by individuals during the past few centuries. The discoverers might not have been aware of the future impacts of their discoveries. Their efforts were purely creative. A few prominent examples would be worth recapitulating.

Johannes Kepler used the then existing observations on planets to propound the Laws of Planetary Motion. These laws have been the starting point from where the present day space science and technology got built up. Pursuit of pure science gave an unintended or unpredicted outcome of benefit to the people. Einstein's Theory of Relativity was a pure scientific contribution. Yet the mass energy equivalence predicted by him eventually provided the clue for development of atomic energy. It also handed over destructive nuclear weapons presently staring menacingly at the mankind. Similarly, discovery of electricity by Michael Faraday has given rise to power industry and motive power for machines, discovery of electron by Thomson has catalysed the growth of electronics industry, discovery of DNA by Watson boosted the development of bio-technology and so on. There are umpteen such examples linking pure scientific discovery to the present day industry or activity that have arisen as a spin-off.

There is also other wider side to this simplistic looking development. The discoveries provided possibilities for ambitious technological missions which needed contributions from variety of scientific and technological disciplines. Such missions provided momentum to organised and integrated tasks of far reaching consequences. Let us take the example of Mission to Moon or other space missions. These needed concentrated efforts to develop new rocket fuels, special materials like ceramics and composites, telecommunication, solar cells, computer based control systems, special foods, special tools, special fabrics and so on. Meeting the functional necessities, and not looking at the costs, was the objective in pursuing these technologies. Yet these new technologies were later found to have potential for use to meet normal human needs. These spin-offs are getting assimilated and commercialised with appropriate adaptations and cost cuttings. The best example is that of satellite communication, television broadcasting, weather forecasting and remote sensing of earth's resources. Special materials are finding many industrial uses such as in aircrafts, automobiles, capital goods, electronics and consumer durables.

Technological breakthroughs out of necessities or inventiveness have eventually found commercial outlets. It has usually taken considerable time and efforts to progress from invention to its commercial exploitation and consumer acceptance. These take-offs are almost fairy-tale stories which have transformed human life. There are many examples to cite. Invention of internal combustion engine lead to industrialisation during 19th and 20th centuries. This was also boosted by the invention of electricity. The motive power provided by the machines and development of variety of industrial products changed the whole lifestyle covering housing, transportation, clothing, food, education, entertainment, employment etc. The complex interplay of different sectors resulted in changes in all facets of human life.

The example of computer is recent and presently being experienced. The motivation for computing was for research and the networking was for defence purposes. The search for semiconducting, magnetic and other electronic materials was out of scientific interests. Combined with engineering of manufacturing techniques, all these efforts lead to rapid developments in computers during the recent past. Finding applications in telecommunication, instrumentation for variety of applications, networking, health-care etc. the computer industry took-off in the past few decades. What was once a research tool has become a gadget of household utility. It also transformed the routinely required services such as banking, trade, various bookings, tax payments, health, education etc. What started as the elitist novelty has become a common utility. Mobile telephony has transited from an elitist to a universal commoner's gadget in a short time span. Computers, mobiles, instruments and allied gadgets are here to stay.

The discovery of DNA over eighty years back was a purely scientific event. Now it is a tool for many applications such as medical diagnosis, crime detection and variety of biotechnology applications. Genomic research, genetically modified foods, use of cloning techniques, production of chemicals and pharmaceuticals etc are just infant steps, setting in the biotechnology age. The impact is already visible in the form of products, processes, treatments and side effects like new ailments and viruses. It is a take-off and one doesn't know where it will take to.

The examples of photocopying and robotics are equally fascinating. What started as innovative ideas to meet felt needs turned out to be universally accepted, viable and useful technologies. It involved long struggle and innovative inputs from different scientific disciplines. Photocopying is now a need of the common man. Robotics is a need of the manufacturing industries, trade and services. Radio, television, photography, mobiles and variety of domestic gadgets are other examples of transition from novelty to universal acceptance.

Scientific discoveries and technological breakthroughs are the success stories of the past couple of centuries. The creativity and innovation have driven these developments. Interplay of disciplines, possibilities of economic benefits, integration and expansion of markets, percolation of knowledge and resulting social integration are the ultimate spin-offs of science and technology. Science in action is found to be beneficial and therefore acceptable. When technology becomes affordable, it is accepted. New knowledge that leads to higher efficiency, productivity and quality, and therefore cost reduction, is accepted. New products such as medicines, surgical techniques and foods are accepted as they are found to be of direct benefit to health and longevity of human being. New knowledge in cultivation of crops, animal rearing and water harvesting is accepted as it helps to raise nutritional status. New knowledge in construction materials and techniques is accepted as it leads to better infrastructure and shelter. So new knowledge is linked to better life and therefore accepted. Growth in agriculture, industry and services has the underlying motivation to improve quality of life. Struggle for new scientific and technological knowledge followed by spin-offs and take-offs changes human life for the better, provided the side effect are well understood and taken care of. Ultimately, value of the tool is decided by the user. Sensible person would put it to best use and prevent misuse. The double-edged sword expects caution in use.

Appetizer for Technology

Any development is linked to adding value to the existing status. If it is economic development, it must be adding value to the goods and services. If it is social development it must be adding value to the social status to raise it to more harmonious/palatable/equitable level. Cultural development accounts for greater opportunity for creative exposition and talent/skill display in a fair societal interaction. Political development depicts greater transparency and fairness in gauging the will of the people. In a way, development is an improvement over the existing value, both subjectively and objectively. This game of value addition is quite crucial, particularly for survival in the competitive environment and improving the quality of existence/life of all as a collective action. Finance, skilled manpower and infrastructure are important inputs for this. However, the most important parameter for value addition in the modern society/economy is the technology.

Technology is linked to cost, productivity and quality of goods and services expected by the people. Particularly, it is a dominating factor in the globalised economy. To meet the market demand for goods and services, inputs of technologies are necessary. In effect, the demand for technology is dependent on the market forces. While the existing market demand has to be met, it is also possible to create new demand as has been experienced during the 20th Century. For example, demand for transport, power, communication, health facilities, education, security etc. are created by new enabling technologies. Enhancement of quality of goods and services could be achieved only by inputs of new technologies and related skills. Education, exposure to new tools, communication and variety of available options are raising the demand for product quality from more people. The resulting competition encourages innovations in technology.

Citizens of a country could be mobilised to generate ambition for development. This requires a leadership of vision and drive. There are success stories of countries, such as Japan and South Korea, coming out of poverty and becoming very strong economies with a high standard of living for its people. This has become possible with strategic initiatives for technological development and assimilation. A strong initiative to develop internal capability for technological change is quite crucial for this purpose. If one looks carefully, every country could find certain internal strengths for faster economic development. Such strengths could include climatic conditions, geographical situation, physical resources, technical skills and overall technological prowess of the country. Some of the traditional skills could be fruitfully utilised if the new technologies are in harmony with those skills. For example, dairy industry in New Zealand, tourism in Caribbean islands, software industry in India etc are prominent successful examples of this type.

Knowing that the technology is crucial for development, it is necessary to understand the dynamics and utility of technology to create a demand for it. It is obvious that the technology will have demand only when the people and enterprises experience its benefits. Developing this appetite for technology in people is important for development. It would be interesting to understand the likely appetisers or incentives or mechanisms for creating demand for technology.

One of the appetiser is seeding of technology. It's a common method in marketing practices to distribute new products to the potential consumers, free or at subsidised cost, to create demand. Many consumer products have been accepted by the people only after testing them in this manner. Food products, soaps, cosmetics and consumer durables have captured markets through such seeding process. New technologies could also be made acceptable by such market seeding process that is making them available on easy terms. Upgrading existing production, starting new productive units, raising income opportunities, cost cutting, improving quality and creating productive employment are major incentives to adopt new technologies. That is in the interest of existing and new entrepreneurs. It would be a good policy initiative by policy makers.

Upgrading of existing technologies and acceptance of new technologies could also be cultivated by introducing suitable standards for products and processes. For example, auto-industry has seen technological upgradation due to introduction of pollution control standards. Food industry has experienced growth due to enforcement of improved quality standards. Similar is the case with metal industry, leather industry, textile industry, electrical gadgets, medicines etc. In essence, the standards for final products could be achieved by upgradation of the process technologies. This also leads to development of allied technical services including tools and skills.

Adopting new productive technologies to start new enterprises and new vocations for becoming competitive and creating income opportunities and employment. Technology has a potential for business growth and higher standard of living. This path of achieving expansion and financial success needs to be projected properly and supported to develop appetite for new technology. Well tried and proven technologies have a better chance for transfer and successful adoption on a wide scale.

A country could develop demand for certain technologies depending on the strategic sectors of the economy. Incentive packages could be developed for specific technologies for their wider adoption. Such incentives could be in the form of tax concessions, subsidies and infrastructural facilities. Technical services, regulatory back-up, administrative support, reliable common utilities, quality control services and overall technology friendly policy regime forms a desirable framework for technology driven development. These are technology promotion initiatives. Incubation of new ideas and technological innovations are important components of this strategy. Entrepreneurship growth and emergence of start-ups are the possible outcomes of such strategy.

All these methods are meant to provide appetiser for adoption of improved technologies by more and more people. It is a desirable policy frame. Creation of demand for technology is the right objective and a correct path for accelerating economic development. It is also an encouragement to innovate and be creative. Many nations have proven that this method works. Hunger for technology is essential to hunt for it. Providing effective appetisers to create this hunger is a need at all times. It is a much needed policy thrust and a chance to come out of the poverty trap and also remain developed. Such policy initiative is in the interest of encouraging entrepreneurship in the people for the common good.

Big is Inevitable

Technology Development, market expansion, economic growth, rising depletion of natural resources and environmental degradation due to a variety of pollutants worked in tandem during couple of decades of the post Second World War period. The resulting environmental concerns raised questions about the very process of development. Schumacher's "Small is Beautiful" paradigm, talk of "Limits to Growth" and the idea of sustainable development propped up during sixties and seventies of the twentieth century. These discussions were intellectually quite stimulating and received enthusiastic support. But this support started waning partly due to emergence of new environment friendly technologies and partly due to globalisation. In fact, the recent trends are shockingly anti-small. Economy of scale is the overriding consideration for cost cutting. The message is quite clear, viz. "Big is Inevitable". It is worth examining the underlying factors.

An upgraded technology inevitably leads to bigger and complex facilities and higher skills. The best example is that of computers and information technology. This fast changing technology has not only led to miniaturisation, but has essentially led to diverse inputs, massive production and service facilities, networks and demand for higher and specialised skills. The process of value addition in any sector leads to bigger and complex facilities, and multitude of skills. This sets a trend towards interdependence, centralisation and enlargement of the complex production system involving intricate supply chain. It also becomes a networked team activity with individuals playing small roles.

Every sector wishes to expand its market. New users and new consumers are tapped to be clients. Globalisation is being propounded and pursued. New services, new products, new crazes, new habits and new addictions are being added to the human needs. The race is on. No one wants to back out and everyone wants to be a winner. New entrants are being encouraged and seduced with fabulous incentives and rewards. Market expansion is a key to commercial success. Reach out, expand or perish is the message. Advantage of scaling up is hammered. Competitive game is on.

Development has also become synonymous with services, enhanced and diverse services. Transport, communication, consumer durables, entertainment, health, banking, education, tourism etc. have become the key parameters to gauge development. Demand for these services is expanding rapidly. Service providers have to expand to match the demand pull. New services are getting added and one has to keep up with the diversity of demands. Mobile communication, internet, social media, networking, e-commerce etc are some of the recent additions to services. Human resource training to meet new needs, infrastructure expansion to tackle the added demands and added services related to improved quality of life and aspirational demands of the younger population.

In the present technology driven expansion, it is quite difficult for any individual to develop diverse skills. Naturally, the option available is that of pooling and integration of complimentary assets and skills. Presently, even the so-called giants have merged to remain competitive in the market. Mergers in auto industry, banking, internet service providers, retail, mobile services, pharmaceuticals etc. are best examples of the recent past. These mergers are critical for survival in the heated competition. These are conscious business decisions of mutual interest. Strategic merger is considered to be the best option to cut costs, tap expanded market and provide new services. Getting bigger is a discernible trend of the modern times.

Technology based services become viable only above a critical size of habitats. The process of urbanisation is linked to viability of demand for services such as communication, health, education, sports, entertainment etc. Small villages remain unviable for such services. They have to merge with urban centres or remain deprived of such services. Speciality hospitals, sports complexes, public transport systems, diverse educational institutions, entertainment outlets, career opportunities etc are viable entities of urbanisation. Similarly, every manufacturing sector have a critical size. With improvements in technologies, critical size of the activity also enlarges. Scaling up is becoming critical for survival in most sectors. This is a natural booster for urbanisation.

Rapid changes in communication technologies, internet services, e-commerce etc. have virtually nullified distances between people. The process of globalisation is on and some enthusiasts are even talking of a global village, a close community. What it means is an interactive, mutually supportive and interdependent community. Here physical distancing is tried to be virtually nullified by communication and information exchange. But it doesn't dismantle the advantages of urbanisation for services and other human activities where physical presence is needed. Urbanisation goes on.

Consumer demands for a large number of commodities could be met by microenterprises. But an expanded market demands macro-level marketing operation. For example, milk production is at micro level. But it's processing and marketing is done at macro level. It calls for backward integration and networking. Many consumer goods call for such integration. The transition from local markets to expanded market is of recent origin, of about 6-7 decades old, and has resulted from technology development, industrialisation and associated urbanisation. The value-added products travel longer distances to reach larger market. It has benefited both producers and consumers. It has made urbanisation attractive.

Technology driven industrialisation and urbanisation has boosted demand for viable diverse services and a very wide network of transport, civic, market, education, housing, recreation and training facilities. The net result is a vast skilled manpower, continuous technology upgradation, rising demands, enlarging facilities, attractive lifestyles and unabated urbanisation. The cycle is complete and self-breeding. Reversal of this trend is not in sight. Opportunities and survival instincts are the driving forces, in spite of difficulties and even urban squalor. Urban to rural transition is just not possible.

Urban centres are the seats of power, both economic and administrative. Their growth is inevitable, in spite of negative consequences like pollution and demand on time. Big businesses are there to stay and further enlarge. Small may be beautiful, but it certainly looks utopian. Big may be ugly or dangerous, but it is inevitable. Small do have a role, but modest one, essentially as a feeder branch. Big is a core activity for progress and prosperity, focal point of multiple opportunities, surely an attraction for the upward moving majority. Big carries the weight, generates demand, aspires to grow and invites attention for multiple actions. No respite from the big and even going bigger. Aspirational forces are pushing the aspirants towards the big, as a viable and sustainable option for survival/progress in spite of bigger costs. Migration towards the big is there to be seen and is unstoppable, on both social and economic counts. It has to be accepted as a clear reality.

Catalysing Sustainable Urbanisation

A study indicates that in the year 1800 A.D., only 3 percent population lived in urban areas. By 1900 it was 14 percent, by 1950 it was 30 percent, by 2020 it was over 50 percent and it may cross 65 percent by 2030. In 1900 A.D., only 12 cities had population over 1 million. By 1950, 83 cities had over 1 million population and this went up to 400 cities by 2020. There were 3 megacities with over 10 million population in 1975, 16 megacities in 2000 and this number is expected to go up to 27 megacities by 2025. The process of urbanisation is going on unabated. It is a natural process cultivated by developments in science and technology. These and associated development lead to a shift from agriculture based rural economy towards urban centric economy driven by industrialisation and growth in services.

By very nature, agricultural economies have to be decentralised. They are based on decentralised local resources, manual labour, deal in barter trade of produce and use traditional skills. Naturally, dispersed rural habitats in proximity to cultivable land and water resources would form the population canvas. Such a rural setting and economic activity creates unviable situation for modern services such as transport, health facilities, banking, education, security etc. In contrast to this, industrial economies cultivate centralisation, tend to enlarge their productive assets for economic viability and in the process breed variety of services such as administration, banking, transport, marketing, education, health, civic facilities etc. Urbanisation is inevitable in such economies. Creation of services also becomes viable due to enlarging size of the urban habitat and its needs. It is a self-expanding set-up. Infrastructure for related services becomes a crying demand of the urbanization. Bigger the city, bigger is the demand for such infrastructure. Even the tertiary services like entertainment, domestic help, maintenance technicians, drivers, security watchmen, lift operators, gardeners, sweepers etc. become sizeable. Bigger the city, bigger is the demand for services, greater viability of services, greater employment opportunities, greater economic activity and all put together, greater rate of growth of the city. City expanding to a megacity is a common phenomenon of the past century in all continents.

Bigger cities are converting the industrial economies into service economies. Such set-ups also create viability for expensive infrastructures such as expressways, metro railways, specialised hospitals, airports, varied educational institutions, sports complexes etc. Bigger the better proves economic sense. But what about environment and quality of life? Are the megacities sustainable, free from mega disruptions and mega disasters? Shouldn't there be an upper limit on city size? What could be the optimum size of a city that could sustain infrastructure of a mega city and yet keeps itself free of ill-effects of a mega city? Such optimum cities could be promoted as countermagnets. The option is worth looking at considering the present urban chaos. Optimum size of the city could be decided on certain criteria, such as the following.

- Availability of land and water, the basic need of the population
- Availability of local road and rail transport for better mobility of the population.

- Feasibility of linkage by road, railway and air to other parts of the country, a need of the business and industry.
- Availability/feasibility of institutions of higher education in variety of disciplines, a requirement of the upward moving middle class.
- Existence of a few major industries or businesses, cluster of medium and small industries or technology parks which provide the core employment and purchasing power to the inhabitants.
- Existence of specialised hospitals and recreational and sports facilities.

Considering these criteria and the present level of urban population density, the minimum size of a viable and attractive city could consist of 1 million population and geographical area of 100 sq.km. Such a size could make all the above criteria feasible and attract investments both in industries and services. The ideal cities would have 2-5 million population with a spread of about 200-500 sq.km. Such a city would provide best of the facilities an urbanite desires, without inflicting the squalor of megacities such as pollution, long travels and unclean conditions. The megacities demand more investments to solve their problems. However, it is observed that such investments, instead, aggravate the problems. In fact, there should be an upper limit on the size of a city. In the populous countries like China, India, USA, Russia, Brazil, Indonesia etc, this limit could be around 10 million population. It is desirable to stop the growth of megacities beyond this limit. In smaller countries this limit could be even lower. The best option is to catalyse viable urbanisation by promoting other urban centres which have the potential for upsizing with all the attractive services and facilities of megacities. What is required to be invested in megacities to solve their current serious problems could be beneficially utilised to promote other attractive urban centres to circumvent these problems.

The most cost-effective option of diverting pressure on megacities appears to be that of urban clustering, wherever naturally feasible. Two or more growing towns within 50 kilometres of each other could be forged into a single cluster and planned to grow towards each other by creating necessary infrastructure such as link roads, local railway network, optimally located airport, industrial growth areas, hospitals, institutions and recreational facilities. Such urban clusters could have the potential to eventually grow into mini megacities in a distant future. Instead of one megacity of 20 million population, 5-10 cities or urban clusters in the population range of 1-5 million could provide better habitat and could be better managed. Such clustering could create attractive urban locations and countermagnets, thus reducing the pressure on megacities. The cost involved would also be much less. Every country and its provinces have these possibilities for implementation over a reasonable period of time. The core amenities would attract private investments in industries, business, institutions, services and housing as a natural process.

The process of clustering could be called as optimum sustainable urbanisation through catalytic investment in core amenities. It would be urbanisation with human face. Similar approach could be feasible to achieve viable ruralisation, clustering of villages to provide viable basic services like water, schools, health centres, transport and communication. Natural processes and expectations, when complimented with policy initiatives, are likely to create humane conditions those everyone has at the back of the mind. What everyone thinks reasonable could become a reality with a united action. It is time to unite for better living conditions for all. If urbanisation is a natural phenomenon, why not give it a human face. It calls for mobilisation of both resources and policy options for feasible, sustainable and attractive outcome in the long run.

Consequences of Competition

In the present charged atmosphere in favour of globalisation, liberalisation, privatisation and open market economic policies, competition and competitiveness have become the buzzwords. It is generally accepted that competition leads to accelerated economic development. The success stories of Japan, Singapore, South Korea and other so-called Asian Tigers have mesmerised the entire world, particularly the developing countries. Developed countries were already in that policy frame and there is nothing new for them as far as open market economies and competition are concerned.

Although a great hype has been created regarding competition, there are a number of questions to be answered regarding its long term effectiveness to bring optimum happiness to the entire society consisting of strong and weak, rich and poor, educated and uneducated, young and old, men and women etc. The population is a complex mixture in any society. Does the competition take care of all the sections in the society? Does the competition and the associated growth bring happiness to the largest fraction of the population? Does the competition cultivate equity? All such questions need to be answered and not just get carried away by the words competition and growth. It would be interesting to know the consequences of competition and being competitive.

Cost Cutting

The most important requirement for a manufacturer to be competitive is to reduce the cost of the product to lure the consumer to buy it. The manufacturer can achieve this by cutting the cost of material inputs, material substitutions, recycling, reducing wastage, inventory control, technological improvements, minimising the cost of capital servicing and efficient marketing of the product.

Another common step is to cut the cost of labour. Labour cost in many manufacturing ventures is quite high. By redeployment of the labour force, adopting labour saving techniques and shifting away from labour intensive technologies considerable cost cutting has been achieved in many industries. Process improvements and optimisations in sectors like minerals, metals, construction, machining, transportation, communication etc have led to cutting in labour costs.

Savings on material inputs and labour are possible through technological upgradation. Technology centred manufacturing processes and services have become a common thrust in the modern industrial set up. This also helps in quality improvements, mass manufacturing of goods and improving services. Naturally this leads to lowering of price that the consumer pays. Scaled-up technologies and large manufacturing set-ups has been a common trend in most of the industrial sectors during the 20th century. Assembly line manufacturing, high degree of mechanisation, robotics and computerised process controls have considerably reduced the cost of products and improved their quality. Naturally more consumers are brought in the net and the overall market expands.

Industry has been quite successful in cutting costs of wide range of products. The markets have expanded and many of the so called elitist products have come within the reach of common consumers. It is no doubt a growth of the economy, but how much of this growth have improved the lives of the people is a nagging question. Growth is also associated with certain adverse effects. Let us look at some of the negative aspects of this growth process.

Negative Effects

The labour saving techniques have led to direct reduction of employment. This is particularly painful in those countries where unemployment/underemployment level is very high. The axe of labour saving invariably falls on unskilled and marginal labour force. Certain section gets further marginalised.

Technology upgradation demands skill upgradation. Naturally only adequately skilled people become employable. They also have to be given higher salaries. So, while unskilled people become unemployed, skilled ones are employed at higher salaries. This leads to an unequal rewards structure unless all are made employable. Most of the developing countries are facing this dichotomy. In a nutshell, competition leads to technology/skill development which further leads to rising inequality in income which further leads to enhanced internal competition to become employable. The net result is anxiety and unhappiness in the society.

If large section of the population is unskilled and unemployable, the competitive economic growth leads to diminishing social returns. No society can sustain excessive inequality. In fact, highly competitive growth results in rising disadvantage to the disadvantaged section of the population. Large section of the population in the developing economies is already disadvantaged on the basis of health, education, location, resources, gender and many other factors. The competition pushes them down further. Where the opportunities are limited, even the normally deserving people may not get reasonable job openings for survival and growth. Under such situation it is very difficult to put blame on them. The threshold levels are too high and the rewards systems are too skewed. Massive unemployment and very stiff competition can only lead to frustration, anger and even anarchy.

In a competitive system, winners get everything. There cannot be too many winners. Average population expects to be provided with average opportunities. If the competition is going to scuttle this basic requirement of the social set-up, it is bound to lead to unhappiness and tension. Most societies face this problem of unequal reward system.

Humane Option

Competition cannot be a panacea for growth in the long run. There has to be an element of sustainability in growth strategy. If the competition is going to create excessive skill bias and income bias, the process would be of a type – two steps forward and one step backward. It would be a creative pruning all along. This needs to be made palatable. Competition need to have a limit, not brutal, fair and based on kind of rules of the enjoyable game. Unless the negative consequences of competition are gauged and controlled properly, competition bubble is bound to burst hurting many. Anything uncontrolled and excessive cannot be sustained for long. Even excessive growth cannot sustain if it is skewed or carries with it excessive and painful inequality. The balance between growth and public action for equity is a need of the time. Every society faces this dilemma and tries to find the way out of the malaise, always in search of a humane touch.

Charity, philanthropy, common cause, graded subsidies, reservations, reforms, social actions, special programmes etc are some of the established methods of giving humane touch to the competitive development. Any deprivation has remained a concern for the society. Restoring balance has always remained a social cause.

Progress Breeded Destruction

Progress is a modern buzzword and also a catchy word to project good intentions and some ideas. Nobody has been able to define it completely. The conflict of interests is clearly visible in different paths suggested by different people to achieve progress. In fact the leaders like to advocate paths which keep their interests intact. One thing is common that advocacy of more and more of everything of benefit or liking means progress. The objectives are linked to money, materials, power, glamour, family, social causes etc. Within one's own psychological boundaries, one likes to maximise any of these possessions or targets. Bank balance, lifestyle, to be in limelight, to be kind/charitable/social or to be an influencer/kingmaker etc. is a choice left to the individual. Yet maximising self-defined, or in the back of the mind, personal interest is the game played by everyone. It is the continuing progress in the set objectives that attracts an individual. No shackles, limits, boundaries or constraints are welcome in the path of progress. Dissatisfaction and unhappiness has to be kept alive to continue progress. Where does this take us individually and collectively?

Progress receives admiration. From a humble hut to a mansion, rags to riches, commoner to a prominent leader, oblivion to eminence are the kind of stories of individual achievements greatly admired and craved for. They only kindle the fire of ambition. Limits and boundaries of diffidence keep losing ground and dreams of progress keep climbing up. More success stories, more attractive goals and the bar of achievements keeps pushing up. Just as technologies get obsolete, ideas also get outdated, innovations are introduced and criteria of progress are redefined. Current level of achievement is aspired to be breached. In most nations, the old basic needs criteria of progress have long surpassed. Services are in demand and even luxuries and superficialities are attracting greater attention. Limits to growth is unacceptable. Nature and natural limits are denigrated as the ideas of the inert and defeatist minds. Think of personal targets and nothing else. Seize the day is the approach. Progress is unstoppable.

Progress hypnotizes everyone. The contents of progress are so seductive that acquiring them is the supreme goal, doesn't matter what means are adopted. Killer instinct is admired. Aggressiveness is applauded. Competition is enjoyed. Defeating the competitor is liked. Outsmarting others with subtle means is uppermost in mind. Everything is fair in love and war is the philosophical justification. Be decisive, show the results, get the job done, no alibis or scapegoats, be a go-getter etc. are the guiding principles to succeed. The whole idea is to overlook means for results. Fairness is a relative term. What is unfair to one could be smartness for the other. Nothing succeeds like success. Yet the overheated system is more likely to reward more unfairness, scheming and one-upmanship. The system gets stronger on techniques and weakens on original or core contents or common good. It keeps losing on sensitivity, morals, inclusive progress and ethics. It is a natural consequence of weakening roots of fair play in a diverse social setting.

At micro level, progress means maximisation of personal interests. It is akin to compartmentalisation of progress. It is competitive segregation of individuals. Over time, it also sets in sectoral imbalance and leaves behind pains of adjustment. The holistic view of common good is somewhat side-lined. Prosperous upcoming sectors prosper further and laggards lag further behind. Gains gravitating towards current winners is a common trend and diminishes basic sensitivity. Accepting such disruption for the sake of accelerated progress is a sure prescription for inequity and disturbing the common good. A sick agriculture sector, diminishing productive sector, large unemployment and underemployment, a few islands of prosperity and glaring inequality is not a healthy sign of progress. Side-lining of broader vision and personal gain dominating in the vast expanse of common squalor is a most disturbing site of compartmentalized progress.

Uncontrolled passion for personal progress generates craze for current sectoral boomers. Careers are selected not based on aptitude and interest, but on the basis of knowledge of current trends. It remains a race for better materialistic opportunities. So everywhere we find few winners and large number of losers. There is no common path of reasonable equity. There is domination of personal craze and no common goal. Defeating the competitor is the goal, and if the winner is going to get everything, then such competition would be destructive in nature. Abundance of losers is a demotivating atmosphere, a simmering discontent and a sure breeding ground for destabilizing activities. The unequal progress only builds frustration and discontent. Can the competition remain healthy? a question that has remained unanswered. Perhaps, competitive progress is an unavoidable natural process of destruction. If man cannot control destructive progress, nature will. Should the man leave it to nature or should he prove that human being is really a thinking animal and seeks balanced common good?

Progress should not imply excess. It is an absurd situation where wants of few keep rising even when basic needs of large section remain unmet. Human being is a part of the organic system called nature. Organic system is a complex system surviving on right proportions of all components in harmony for long run sustenance. It contains checks and balances. It looks for optimum and not for maximum. It abhors imbalance. Greater the imbalance, greater is the reaction. Mutinies and revolutions in human history are typical corrective actions to imbalance. There are examples of fast moving economies getting embroiled in disturbing situations which partially undo the achievements. Environmental degradation, rise in criminality, wasteful lifestyles, social unrests etc. are some of the negative elements of progress. There are corrective measures to tackle uncontrolled material progress. Variety of economic, administrative and legal measures are designed to control imbalance and facilitate equity. These may sometimes appear dampeners to progress, but they seem essential for long term sustainability. Above all the very democratic process that provides opportunity for course correction helps in avoiding excesses in societal path to progress.

It has become necessary to redefine progress. The glamour of maximum needs to be replaced by pragmatic optimum. Progress needs to be sustainable and inclusive. Creating opportunities to all needs to be the objective and not cultivate a situation of fierce competition to project a few winners and many losers. Having a few performers and many observers is an unhealthy sign. Merit flourishes in opportunities. Excessive competition only breeds schemers and operators. Optimum competition, comparable rewards or compensations, strong movement towards common good and process of inclusion needs to be the basis of progress. This would make the life less painful, ensures broader involvement, follows balanced reward system and remains in harmony.

Of course, it would have less of glitter, grandeur, elegance, scintillation, fascination and by far less exclusivist. High time to realise that the progress should not breed destruction of humane touch. After all, progress essentially means higher level of enlightenment and wellbeing of all.

Professions and Sensitivity

From caves to organised society, the human transition has taken thousands of years of evolutionary efforts. It is a transition from survivalistic self-sufficiency to progressive interdependence. Drawing on services of others to meet multiple individual and community needs is the basis of modern societal life. Various professions emerged over time to provide these services. Government, agriculture, education, trade, medical, energy, transport, communication, construction, security, defence, legal, banking etc. are the services needed for sustaining societal life. These are the services for humans provided by humans. These are knowledge and skill based services with increasing specialisations and training requirements. Human life has certainly become complex, demanding and highly interdependent. How much conscious are the professionals in providing the expected services to their fellow beings? The picture is quite confusing.

The process of selection of professions itself is beset with contradictions. Professional preferences generally come to light during the time of admissions to various courses. School education remains liberal with some scope for testing inclinations of the students. In the fierce competition, current trends for professions are looked into by the students and the parents. The single most important criterion applied is that of employment possibilities and earning potential of the profession. Aptitude, skill, liking and ability get a back seat. Sensitivity and attachment towards the professional service and commitment towards the served get the last consideration. The language of justification is usually loaded with expectations of financial rewards or money making possibilities. Jumping on the current bandwagon is a craze for the most, a herd mentality. Medical, engineering, management, finance and now computer bandwagons have rolled during the past five-six decades. Important early professions like agriculture, teaching, defence services, scientific research, legal services and civil services have lost their glamour/élan. Yet these core professions can never become irrelevant at any stage. Only that these have gone low on choice.

Glamour of money spinning professions has a negative influence on other professions in the form of reduced interest and low on commitment. Naturally this affects sensitivity towards the served. When money becomes overriding objective, even the traditional professions look for unscrupulous methods to make money. Sensitivity towards the served declines. Tricks are attempted to acquire the missing glamour. So we get into a situation where a doctor exploiting patient, a teacher not helping or guiding the students free, a public servant not caring about the public grievances, an engineer not putting his heart into his project and doing a sloppy job, contractor compromising quality, lawyer squeezing the client, police ignoring the troubled or victims and so on. Those to be served are ignored or exploited.

Using professional skill and position for exploitation is not only insensitive but against professional ethics. Highly unequal reward structure and frequent emergence of new bandwagons has created a situation where reasonable equity is lost and making money mind-set creeps into all professions. Those who can't make money get frustrated and simply don't care about their jobs. Only a small percentage does remain committed to their professions and give their best in any situation. They have chosen their profession out of liking and interest and less for rewards. Professional ethics demand problem solving attitude and being useful. To serve is considered noble and there should be a pleasure in the job to be done. Anything devoid of this attitude only leads to loss of professional ethics. Ill-treatment of animals in Zoos or on farms, disabled in orphanages, deprived, subordinates etc is a typical example of professional insensitivity. Treating of patients without proper diagnosis is not uncommon. Bureaucratic delays has become a common feature in the public service, making public to suffer. Teacher not teaching or helping or inspiring the students is nothing but downgradation of education to a great extent. Politicians and civil servants keeping personal benefits uppermost in minds is experienced as a painful reality. Exploiting those to be served is clearly an unethical practice. The trends are quite disturbing.

When the professions are selected for their money potential, other important factors such as commitment and interest are pushed aside. The working gets trapped in superficialities, glossy words, cosmetic outfits such as modern gadgetry and showy methods. The substantive part of the work is side-tracked and tried to be glossed over with what could be termed as supplementary things. One easily feels the ascending superficiality in action. For example, one may be computer literate, but if command over the language itself is poor the resultant communication would be inadequate. A nicely decorated office may not provide nice service and quality output. A doctor using modern instruments may not diagnose the patient correctly. A well-dressed teacher may not teach well. A public servant with all facilities may not be helpful to the people. A scientist with best instruments may not produce original or innovative work. From all these examples, the point to be noted is that without interest and commitment, the core of the professional service or output may be missing in spite of all the wherewithal, inputs and environment.

In the race for money, cosmetic gloss and showmanship, what remains is a professional insensitivity and poor service. Building professional competence and insight are often ignored. In the process, creativity is undermined and innovativeness gets suppressed. Without creativity and innovation no service could be adequate and no profession could improve. Straitjacketing of profession in routines, rules and superficiality is detrimental to its growth in the long run. Only mundane administration would get ascendancy. Administration, which is supposed to be a facilitating service provider, becomes the major beneficiary of the profession at the cost of the professional objective itself. Administration becomes the ruler and not a facilitator. This is a problem with most of the developing societies. Where administration rules, professional output and its quality, effectiveness and modernisation are bound to suffer. Coming out of this dichotomy needs to be the priority.

Professionals should rise to the occasion and restore the nobility of their professions. There is a need for ascending sensitivity in the professionals. They should bring the customers/beneficiaries/served at the centre-stage of their activities. What is needed is a caring doctor, helpful public servant, inspiring teacher, sensitive politician, innovative scientist, committed engineer and so on. Delivering professional output need to be the core objective. Any dilution in it is insensitive, unethical and against the basis of professionalism.

Perhaps, in majority cases, professions are not chosen out of interest. Choice made is low on priority, out of situational compulsions, being in the lower side of the social pyramid, not having enough opportunities to rise in the ladder of merit, having some form of handicap or simply being underprivileged. Nobody could be blamed for this. Circumstances have just got insensitivity thrust in the professions. Only motivated succeed in crossing this threshold and provide yeomen service to the served, even in the adversities and demotivational atmosphere all around. Such single minded motivated ones do exist and are there to see, doing the best whatever they do.

Motivating Leadership

A look into the history shows a large number of unique individuals who could generate massive following and bring about historical changes. This has happened in all facets of human life including social, political, economic, religious, cultural and professional fields. Movements for freedom from foreign rule, movements against discrimination, movements for economic growth, democratic governance, labour movements, gender reforms, religious movements etc. are historical actions lead by unique leaders. Such leaders have emerged in all parts of the globe. These movements have made profound impact on societal evolution. The common feature of these leaders is their ability to motivate a large section of the population. In fact, the quality of leadership, its strength and its effectiveness primarily depends upon its ability to motivate the concerned section of the population. In the modern context, the quality of leadership of an organisation or institution or business or charity could be gauged by its ability to motivate the members of that organisation. Such a motivating leadership needs to be understood in a right perspective.

Motivation is a state of the mind by which an individual desires to act in a particular situation. Depending upon the situation his/her action to perform emerges. It could be an instruction to be followed or a decision to be taken or routine acts to be performed, it is the inner inspiration that decides the action. Such inspired actions or motivation strongly influences individual's performance in a given situation. The motivating factors could include financial and material incentives, power to wield, family influences, social pressures, cultural influences, personal likings, personality assets, influences of unique individuals etc. The influencing factor is individual specific. In organisational and societal settings it is the influence of leadership that decides the motivation of the people involved.

In a big organisation such as government, military, institution, bank or large industry, normally a pyramidal structure exists. Different levels of functions are assigned. A good leadership would motivate individual functionary to take decisions and perform in the best interest of the organisation. In the absence of such environment, individuals would only keep looking up for directions. Motivating subordinates to act and do their jobs is a function of the leader. Establishing mutual confidence is an essential element of this function. A credible leadership can instil such confidence. Motivation is generated out of confidence building measures, delegation of powers, non-interference, trust and support.

Motivating leadership creates enthusiasm and hopes, something to look forward to. This raises the level of performance of the organisation benefiting everyone. Lethargy is shaken, irritants are pushed aside, pettiness is given up and the resulting positive actions harmonise to bring best out of the organisation. Personal gains are looked at within the parameters of common good. The leadership instils the realisation that survival and betterment of the organisation is paramount even for personal gains. Everyone is lifted with the organisational high tide. The leadership shows the way by own actions, behaviour and guidance. The in-built fairness and inspirational atmosphere in the organisation benefits everyone. Nobody feels left behind.

No individual can lead in all situations. One is tailored for certain situations. Mahatma Gandhi could lead a non-violent freedom movement in India. Nelson Mandela could lead a non-violent movement against apartheid in South Africa. Contrary to this someone like Winston Churchill could lead violent war efforts against military aggression in Second World War. Similarly, leading a business, an institution, a team etc. are different endeavours meant for different types of individuals. Contents, means and parameters would be different, but the common underlying requirement is the ability to motivate those being lead. Leader should lead, a motivating force for all involved to do their job well and succeed. Leading from the front is the essence of good leadership. It is building trust, creating harmony, mobilising strengths and motivating the followers.

Those who cannot motivate cannot lead. A person with personal agenda, self-centred behaviour and negative motives cannot lead. Not many would follow such a person for long. A spoiler cannot lead as others would be scared of the outcome. A crook can be a leader of crooks and cannot lead the common man who is normally decent and innocent. A cynic usually drives everyone away and is close to none. An arrogant cannot lead as no one likes to be insulted. Coercive, abrasive or authoritarian leader is disliked by most, unless endowed with some special qualities giving unique performance. Shrewd, tricky and manoeuvring type of leader is dealt with cautiously in an atmosphere lacking openness and fresh air. Cool and calculating leadership is respected, but is not good enough for stirring performance. It is acceptable in much civilised conditions. Disciplinarian leadership with conviction and action is enigmatic and generally feared. It is acceptable in societies beset with diversities and frictions. Leadership centralising power is generally not liked unless there exists a compelling situation. All these traits are quite common and put limitations on the nature and quality of leadership. There can be no perfect leader. Only the situation makes the leader successful or otherwise.

Knowledgeable, positive, self-disciplined, liberal, value-based and generous leadership is generally liked and respected. It is normally inspiring, operates on strong common sense, delegates power and in all probability could forge unity in diverse following. It has higher credibility and could tune the organisational atmosphere for better performance. It motivates discipline, honesty and action amongst the followers without resorting to force. Diversity is an essential element of sustainability, a balancing force, a smoothening complementarity. Bringing harmony amongst the diverse functions for common good is what a good leadership is supposed to do. Identifying diverse talent and using it appropriately is what leaders are expected to achieve. That is the motivating leadership, likely to give the best possible performance. In reality, it is rare to find, and a great luck to come across, such leadership.

Finding a suitable leader has always been a problem. For governing a country, democratic processes have been fairly successful and got well rooted during the past century. Leadership for businesses are gradually shifting from family-based to professional. Cadre driven and merit-based selection criteria are getting prominence in institutions and varied services. Domain expertise and special skills are becoming necessities in specialised leadership roles. So the diversity of needs in specialised activities calls for cultivating expertise driven leadership in narrow domains. Protocols are getting evolved for such leadership selection. For example, mechanisms are well in place for selection of heads of universities, colleges, laboratories, courts, hospitals, financial institutions and so on. Merit to lead and ability to motivate the team cannot be ignored. Ultimately, the leader has to understand the task to be performed and deliver results.

Championing Simplicity

Most people prefer simplicity in day-to-day life. Given an option, they would try to remain away from complexity as botheration is generally disliked. Smooth and unhindered activity is what everyone likes. People are basically peace lovers or commoners looking for reasonably happy life, struggling to survive without much hassles. Those who have creative instincts are focused and like to be unto themselves, keep working for their goals. Any diversion is not liked. There are also nature lovers who advocate non-interference in nature. They resist any kind of artificiality and prefer to live in harmony with nature. Similar is the case with environmentalists who champion the cause of protection of environment, biodiversity conservation, maintaining natural habitat and sustainable use of natural resources. So unless coaxed by some compelling reasons, one likes to be simple.

Minimizing complexity, everyone speaks about, but very few are able to keep it that way. Rules and regulations keep adding with time, thanks to emergence of new vocations, new professions and new possibilities of mischiefs. Progress and modernisation pushes up rules of the game, diversity of needs and new seductive wants. The march of complexity is unstoppable. Take the simple case of automobile. Bicycle to motorbike to automobile to sedans to SUVs to limousines, the journey of private transport is breathtakingly fast. Technology has improved, but overall inefficient or wasteful and excessive use of natural resources is a glaring reality. Mobile telephone growth is phenomenal, but wasteful communications have gone up, diversions are causing inefficiency, exposure to junk information is dangerously intrusive and disruptive usage is a cause for concern. Simple and pleasing and honest ways of life are under strain and much disturbed, raising more worries to deal with. Things like trolling, use of offensive language, mobilisation of antisocial activities, cybercrimes, frauds etc are bothering everyone and also putting much stress on the law and order machinery. So with pluses, minuses have also gone up. Ease in life has suffered and is receding.

The complexity is not an artificial creation. It is a part of the natural process of evolution and development. The so called progress is associated with complexity as the new parameters and new dimensions are added to the way of life. More tasks are added, more demands creep in, more specialisations keep adding and the human activity keeps getting complex. These are natural additions, demand based and often blind to the consequences. The voice of few who understand the negative side is drowned in the euphoric acceptance of progress. Complexity is a natural bandwagon rolled out of progress, seductive due to the outer sparkle of benefits, and everyone tries to jump on. The attraction of progress is beyond control. Simplicity remains on the back seat, ignored and goes unnoticed. Besides, human crazes of various kinds add to the complexity.

With new knowledge and new techniques becoming available, there is a natural craze for using them for getting competitive edge. Raw natural talent alone is not enough to win. Every competition is becoming an exercise to find methods of winning. Techniques are acquired by taking special efforts, training, coaching and guidance. Preparatory work, special booster diets, medical help and honing the techniques is becoming a big business now. Those who can afford to get this back-up are in an advantageous position. It does cost money, time and energy which very few may be able to mobilise. Big achievers, though talented, often have supplemented it with big coaching back-up. Competitions have become a game of techniques and strategies to get enough edge that is needed to win and earn big. It is also an outcome of skewed reward system that the modern progress has introduced in the form of big monetary gain and public focus for winners. Big cost obviously expects big return and vice-a-versa. So competitive games and entertainment formats have not remained hobbies, but have become full-time professions, a craze for young and ambitious. But few big winners also create vast number of losers, a reality to be kept in mind while deciding to pursue the craze.

Craze for one-upmanship, showmanship, ego satisfaction do add to complexity. One likes to be a psychological winner. I am better than you, a psychological game most like to play. In professions, politics, social reforms, sports etc, personal performances and contributions are tried to be projected as better than others to gain advantage. Marketing self or product or brand or service is an objective for all those who are in the race of one-upmanship. Showmanship is practiced by those who are not only in show business, but also by those who crave for exclusivity. A showman may choose an odd dress to draw attention, the political class may adopt attire that is commoner friendly and yet special, the executives may don branded apparels, the socialites prefer designer dresses, the religious preachers have their peculiar choice of cloths, like robes and caps, and so on. Similarly professions like military, police, medical services, legal services etc are identified with their uniforms and add-ons. These are evolved choices to differentiate from others.

Ego is a part of the human character. To satisfy ego, a variety of methods are adopted. Famous are the acquisition of exclusive items like expensive vehicles, entertainment systems, ornaments, houses, dresses, furnishings and so on. To prove status, protocols and hierarchies are followed meticulously by many. Anger, sarcasm, gestures and postures are commonly used for ego satisfaction. All these crazes are obviously at the cost of simplicity. More of these only add to complexity of existence.

The craze for power is visible at all levels and in all professions. Rising in the hierarchies and gaining more power is liked by most. Higher positions, many strive to get by any means. Using powers for good work, personal gains as also to settle scores with others is a common practice. Race is on. Besides the pleasure and excitement, position is also associated with an element of mistrust, fear, tension, stress etc in dealing with subordinates as well as superiors. Yet, the control and the leverage that one gets with power is enjoyable to most. Wielding power, settling scores, doing favours, bossing, perks etc are diverse benefits one gets from power. There is in-built liking for these benefits, besides the monetary gains. Glamour of power is a craze, though infected with complexity.

Progress with knowledge growth, bulging competition, greater aspirational avenues, craze for success and gains are there to stay. The resulting diversion from the core objective of normal, simple and peaceful life is happening as a natural outcome. The process is heading towards more complexity. The raw natural performance is overtaken by grilling, techniques and protocols, anti-thesis of simplicity. Amateurism and hobby is overtaken by professionalism. Simple natural talent is overwhelmed by complex professional bandwagon of techniques. Mastering techniques is becoming more important and inevitable than natural talent assets. It is a natural discrimination between haves and have-nots. Obviously, championing simplicity is a big challenge in an atmosphere that is clearly headed away from nature. Going back to nature is an uphill task, like moving against the stream. Simplicity is slipping away, providing royal passage to complexity to creep in. Are we aware of the hidden loss?

Sustaining an Idea or a Mission

Curiosity exists in every individual. New ideas, new visions, new tasks, new missions etc do emerge from human mind. To get them in practice is, however, an uphill task. Very few of these see the light of the day, are tried to be acted upon and a very miniscule number survive and sustain. Where things go wrong? Why so called good initiatives fail to survive? Well meaning, well intentioned ideas just get degenerated and eventually die. Is it a human problem or a problem with the idea itself? Answer is not simple, but definitely it is a combined effect of human factors, shortcomings in the idea itself, ill-conceived action and changes in situation with time. In a way, everything is likely to be half-cooked, not matured enough, needs changes with time, faces nature's hurdles, faces challenges of relevance and finds itself in flux with sustenance remaining in doubt.

History is full of examples of creative initiatives of individuals. Institutions have been created, organisations have been set up and movements have been established in a mission mode by individuals and/or groups. These are constructive activities of benefit to the people, although there are examples of destructive ideas also. Creation of religions, civilizations, empires, explorations of new lands, languages, art, education, architecture, agriculture, medicine, science, technology, finance, manufacturing, democracy, governance, public institutions and so on, the list of ideas in action is unending. Seeding of idea, establishing its need, making it survive and grow and sustain it is generally out of efforts of a few unique individuals, the pioneers. Such examples are there to be seen. Yet its survival is primarily linked to its acceptance by the people. With time, if the acceptance level comes down, the idea and its outcome gets into decline mode. New ideas take their place.

If we look at institutions, organisations and movements, we find that many of these are linked to individuals for creation. The originators create them, sustain them during their lifetime and if they fail to establish sustenance mechanism, decline of these creations is inevitable. Often these creations achieve their objective and lose their relevance for existence. Some are replaced with better options in tune with the time. Movements like freedom from foreign rule, racial equality, religious freedom, voting rights, gender equality, collective bargaining, freedom of expression, democracy etc started and by and large succeeded. Often the movements, as they start declining, change the formats and continue in low key, if they must. So, for example, racial equality and gender equality though legally achieved, still continue to remain as issue for other smaller elements such as pay parity, fair treatment and lingering discrimination. Passionate anchors of the movements continue to raise these issues and keep pursuing.

Creating something new by the originator and sustaining it by later anchors is a job that needs complete dedication to the cause. Such leadership is rare and demands a unique character. It has to show a passion for change, change to overcome continuing inequity, change towards equality of opportunity, change for freedom of choice and so many other core human principles. Somebody coming forward to change discriminatory traditions and doggedly face the resistance from the existing beneficiaries needs not only the courage of conviction but also face the personal risk of isolation. Such originators and reformers have shown strength and tenacity of personality, not to give up and single-mindedly work for the goal. Obviously such personalities have attracted supporters and co-workers to join and anchor the task later with dedication.

Credibility of the originators/founders is found to be very high. This credibility is a combination of many elements worth looking at. Generally the task taken in hand is a need of the time, beneficial to a sizeable section of the population and is in the direction of undoing some prevailing wrong or shortcoming. The issue may be simmering for long, be well articulated, but waiting for an innovative and credible action. Inertia busting and driving the desired change is a task cut out for the motivated. It involves risk taking and perseverance. It is also a task needing high level of intelligence, insight, intuition and innovation. It is a mission to be achieved with integrity. The originator is essentially a trustworthy prime mover. In a broader sense, he/she is the architect of the movement or the creation. During the struggling period, like the pioneer, the followers are also motivated, dedicated, passionately willing to perform and not looking for exploiting, not for glamourizing and nor for trivializing the task taken in hand. These are creative minds with focus on broader wellbeing. A long pending and long haul battle to be won.

The followers anchor the change in the long run. They are not in the limelight, nor are they in hunt for personal benefits. They are silent workers, quietly doing their job. Such unassuming lot do a better job. They are like dedicated volunteers, follow the leader and don't hanker for positions. A leader is required to inspire and guide, but the team is a necessity for performance. Be it literacy, labour welfare, racial reforms, gender equality, civil liberties, freedom of choice etc, these movements have achieved positive change due to the silent workers, the unsung heroes. No reformer/leader has failed to acknowledge this contribution of the followers to the change.

Danger exists in dilution of dedication over a period of time, as personal interests start encroaching after the initial successes and as struggles start getting milder. The movements/institutions start losing relevance and punch of the initial phase. It is a time for new ideas to emerge. The fact remains that generation of new ideas is a societal need. New problems prop up needing new ideas to deal with. Creativity is in demand forever. New ailments, new skills, new demands, new problems like climate change, new explorations and revelations are unstoppable outcomes of human activity. New ideas are bound to be churned out to deal with new demands. Sustaining ideas remains a challenge. But the fertile human mind finds it worth facing a challenge and try to succeed. Pioneers have to emerge and show the new paths those have a better chance to sustain.

With knowledge build-up over the past couple of centuries, particularly in science and technology, new avenues as well as problems have propped up. Technological applications have led to growth and urbanisation. The nature of problems has changed providing new challenges to deal with, needing bigger organised actions. Issues like security, economic growth, social stability, employment, complexity of governance etc are undergoing fast changes. Influence of technology is clearly visible with fast changes in various fields of activity. With changing times, new ideas and new missions are bound to emerge needing new leaders and anchors.

Platitudes vs Performance

Broad views, generic statements, poetic language, firm opinions etc are often lose talks of less consequence and more of venting inner feelings based on casual thinking. Nothing much is expected out of these expositions. These platitudes are more for passing the time, to show presence and to project separate identity. It has nothing to do with actual performance or any utilitarian output. So long as nobody asks for performance, people like to give wide opinions and advice. It is a common experience of non-experts criticising experts, leaders being drubbed by citizens, executives being confronted by hostile subordinates and so on. It is worth looking at the casual versus responsible positions in our normal working.

There exists a big gap between theory and practise, even though both are important. Theoretical understanding of a topic is one thing, but to use it in practice, many other issues are involved. Take the case of education. If developing cognitive capability of a child is a theoretically sound objective of education, to deal with the large number of diverse students in a structured format, need arises for many compromises related to curriculum content, teacher's role, evaluation method, parents' involvement, economic inputs, social structure, job opportunities, skill requirements and so on. Similarly, use of scientific principle for useful technology development needs consideration of economic viability, market demand, consumer choice etc. Sound economic development principles may have to be tailored to accommodate the elements of equity, possible misuse, environment, political differences, long term vision, structural limitations etc. Social reforms demand consideration of human, locational and economic parameters. Practicing principles calls for sound judgement and sensitivity towards diverse human needs, with focus on optimum common benefit. This is where the leadership plays a crucial role.

All ideas do not get converted into practice or a product. Very few flights of imagination find the light of the day. Whether it is scientific invention or social engineering or economic reform or political strategy, new ideas may not work all the time. People keep trying without success or desired outcome. Ideas are often half-cooked, beset with narrow track thinking, unaware of other related parameters influencing the outcome and lacking commitment to overcome the unknowns. Idea to useful output is a learning process needing course corrections, trial and error method and a practical exercise. It needs persuasion and open mind to carry out necessary changes on the way. Success stories of inventors, reformers, entrepreneurs and politicians are loaded with such persuasion and hard work.

The general tendency of looking at problems in a philosophical angle without aiming for a practical action is rather an irresponsible attitude. Even if importance of developing broad perspective is accepted, that cannot be the end objective. What is expected is a specific line of action. This may involve compromises and clear understanding of practical limitations on implementation of an idea. Philosophizing a problem does not mean advising without taking responsibility of implementation. Those who do the job need to have freedom to make choices for specific action. Opinion makers and philosophical thinkers do have a role, but doer's role is more valuable, difficult, risky and responsible. Giving opinion is easy and most of the times turns out to be a loose talk, irresponsible to the core. Doers are likely to have vested interests, but they also take responsibility of performance. Philosophical and doer is a rare combination, a sound practitioner giving desired output. There is a need of such performers.

There is no dearth of advisors, often providing unsolicited advice to all and sundry and on any subject. Such persons are unlikely to accept challenges of actual work. For them actual work is somebody else's job. Politicians in power, public servants and service providers are often the targets of criticism as they are supposed to show work done. On the other hand, opinion makers, armchair intellectuals, journalists, writers, free wheelers, socialites and inheritors of cosy lifestyle are often in the forefront to give advice. Debates on public issues are usually loaded with advice. Those who have to carry out the actual work have to make a choice from the advices and feasibility of implementation, a tough task.

Persons in distress, handicapped, losers and unlucky ones have to move on in their life with own means and with grit. Outside help or no help, they have to face the challenge. They may get good amount of sympathy and support, but that cannot be guaranteed forever. Many may be willing to shed crocodile tears for them, provide advice and extend some help. This could meet only partial need, give psychological relief and show a way forward. However, by and large, the onus of actual task remains with the affected person to move on. Self-help is the ultimate savoir.

Advice is often associated with platitudes. Talking hollow and showing off is a pastime for many. It is inconsequential and ends at that. From theoretical generality to specific action is a difficult transition that few can make. It needs not only understanding of the parameters involved, but also integrity and willingness to act and to take responsibility for the consequences. Good professionals and committed individuals do show this quality, attitude and confidence. They are unassuming workers with clarity of objectives, positive in action and have willingness to deliver.

Talking in air and big, without substance, has an element of deception. It lacks seriousness and willingness to be useful. It may be a camouflage for a hidden personal agenda. Whatever may be the motive, platitudes without substance is an undesirable method in a civilized society. The mistrust and negativity that it generates does more harm in the long run. On the other hand, robust honesty as a core value brings more benefits to all. It sets the benchmark for common interests overriding personal interests. Honesty in public service, economic activities, business, professions, family life etc is, in all likelihood, expected to be more beneficial in raising the quality of life of all.

People resorting to double speak, or uninvolved, are a confused lot with no clarity of objectives. It is a method of playing safe, not being committal and not taking risk. It also shows an element of timidity in judging a situation. Not leading from the front cannot be a policy of the courageous and the wise. Similarly, jumping for taking credit and unwillingness to accept mistakes is unlikely to help anyone. It would generate only a rat race to be non-committal and uninvolved, essentially side-lining core values of common good. This isolationist and aloofness syndrome benefits none.

Irresponsible platitudes need to give way for commitment to perform. Half-hearted, hollow, deceptive, double speak and non-committal lose talks only create hurdles. These should be discouraged. Implementers need to be given freedom to deliver. The performance and credibility of the implementers is at stake. Ultimately integrity, commitment, freedom and performance have to go together to keep hurdles of platitudes at bay. Field day to lose talks is bound to undermine performance, not in the interest of the people.

Looking to Deliver Results

What is theoretically correct may not be fully valid in practise. Dilution sets in depending on the feasibility of an idea. In practise, interests of all don't match for a variety of personal reasons and situational variations. Balancing these interests to optimise the outcome, justifiable compromises are made. Inadequacy of theoretical position is usually realised as the conflicting interests to be accommodated are often based on ignorance. Theory projects an ideal position that is never available in reality, particularly in those cases where human being is involved. By and large, human behaviour is unpredictable. So, in a given situation, there is a wide variation in behaviour of individuals, including completely opposite positions. Even common basic values like honesty, integrity, discipline, respect, merit, equality etc, though theoretically sound, do not get universally entrenched due to mismatch or ignorance driven personal interests. Practising needs compromising. Eventually everything gets aggregated or averaged out to an all-inclusive acceptable level.

In all activities, people involved do get new ideas to improve the work output. In most cases, however, these ideas remain ideas and do not find acceptance in practise as these may not be acceptable to all. In fact, idea to innovative product or practice is a big shift that remains un-fructified. Failure is typically linked to many practical aspects such as utility, economic viability, technical limitations, end-user response etc. Converting idea into something acceptable is a big challenge that is faced across the activities and communities. So, throwing up idea is easy, but taking it to fruition is a different cup of tea. It needs much higher application of mind, deep understanding of the practical issues, assessing available choices, conducting trials, adopting extensive persuasion or use of high pressure methods. Bringing change or reforms is not easy.

Philosophical posturing is a common pastime which many enjoy. Taking a high moral ground, talking about policies with which one is not directly concerned, commenting on performance of others, speaking on unknown and unrelated matters etc are typical methods people adopt in an attempt to put themselves on a higher pedestal. Such positioning is inconsequential as they know they are not expected to prove it in practice. Philosophising an unconcerned issue is not only irresponsible but also hypocritical. Those who wish to perform need to be specific and firm in action. Balancing conflicting interests in deciding specific action may be a compromise and in conflict with philosophical position. Such situations do arise in disputes within family or between organisations, social groups, communities, countries etc and the emerging action may be a compromise between conflicting philosophies. Philosophical positioning have inherent limits in real life situations. To be practical means compromising, accommodative and positive.

Giving advice is liked by people, even if it is not solicited. Such unsolicited advice is generally not liked by those to whom it is directed. This is often experienced in case of parents advising wards, teachers advising students, seniors advising juniors, predecessors advising successors, elders advising youngsters etc. People like to be left alone in making choices and taking decisions. Besides ego, following one's own chosen path is the idea in not taking anyone else's advice. Often, giving advice is easy, but doing the actual work is difficult. Advice is normally infected with platitudes and lose talk. Doing a job needs dealing with realities. In fact, in most cases, people don't need advisors, they need workers. Focused advice linked with expertise or experience may be desirable and professionally essential. Similar is the case with advice from mentors and well-wishers. However, lose and irresponsible advice is an avoidable burden to be set aside.

Motives behind giving unsolicited advice could be many. In advice to losers or depressed, approach is to show sympathy and desire to share the pain, akin to shading crocodile tears. Motivational statements provide only momentary relief and the impact is ignorable, irrelevant or even may be irritating. In case of public causes like environment, security, health, education etc, advice is quite common and doesn't go beyond show-off and hollowness. Public causes are quite challenging and risky, and very few venture to take up these and work for them. So, we find many talking about environment, deprivations, handicaps, disparities etc but very few may be actually contributing to overcome the related problems. Advice turns out to be doublespeak, if it is based on ignorance. Lack of clarity leads to generalities, half-truths, misguiding, confusing everyone involved. It may not make any positive contribution or be helpful. In fact, it may do more harm to the receiver.

Advice could have hidden agenda. There is likely to be an angle of deception, if advice is used to push personal agenda. Use of superlative words in misplaced praise, talking big to misguide, posturing goodwill to camouflage crooked moves, friendly gestures to buy time, providing wrong information etc are some of the deceptive moves adopted to gain advantage. They lack honesty and are usually looked at with suspicion. There is credibility gap. On the other hand, honesty is taken seriously, respected and seen to be in wider interest. Honesty doesn't need crutches of platitudes, superlatives and philosophies. It is simple, straight, credible and to the point. Its focus is on performance and tangible benefits to all concerned. It needs courage of conviction and clean action.

Resorting to hollow statements is a sign of irresponsibility. Buying time with such talks for personal agenda is not in wider interest. It undermines performance and output. On the contrary, commitment to performance is the responsible way of doing a job at hand. Anything substantive could be achieved with more commitment and less of loose talks. There are examples of unassuming and committed social workers, teachers, scientists, administrators, professionals, businessmen, artists, sportsmen etc who have done creative work of benefit to the people, and that even at personal loss. Integrity that they have shown needs to be appreciated. In fact, they are the unsung heroes as they never tried to project themselves and remained away from hogging the limelight. For this, they must have no regrets as they were driven by commitment, possessed with integrity, held passion to perform and delivered benefits to others. These are commendable attributes and can never be matched by those addicted to hollow talks, howsoever mesmerising they may appear.

Theoretical mooring, idea generation, philosophical base and will to act may form the foundation for a useful output. However, there has to be a limit to theorising. Too much of it without showing commensurate performance is nothing but a waste of energy and rather a disservice. So there has to be balance between theorising and tangible output. Let feet be firmly on ground, integrity the guiding force and performance the primary objective. Ultimately, honesty and performance together is admired.

Priming Body and Mind

Individuals are different, their characteristics are different, their life spans are different, their performances are different, their problems are different, their strengths are different and so on. Shaping of personalities and activities performed depend on complex factors. One thing is certain that this shaping depends on the training to the body and mind, even knowingly or unknowingly, during the life span. This exercising of body and mind happens in a variety of ways, through outside inputs as also through self-motivated actions. The outcome could be anything like exciting or dull or satisfying or painful, depending upon the preparations, circumstances and luck.

There are multiple methods to give exercise to body and mind. Early childhood gets most inputs from parents and close ones. Free movements in early growth and picking up gestures, sounds and words takes place during this period. Later childhood experiences greater interactions and gets wider inputs to pick up new skills, physical strength, language and diverse knowledge base. The period of youth provides freedom to acquire structured inputs to set up careers and professional objectives. Plenty of choices and advisories pour in to choose from and it forms a struggling period. What shape the body and the mind would take depends on the personal capability and circumstances. The adulthood is a completely self-made period that shapes professional progress, family formation and social participation. During this period, body and mind are mostly self-governed with full responsibility. Any shortcoming is personal and rectifying action is also personal. Having passed the professional and family pressures, oldies have to take care of themselves, may be with some assistance from others, needing appropriate reshaping of body and mind. In case of ill and handicapped, the inputs for shaping mind and body are expected to be somewhat different from the normal. Special routines and methods have to be added to take care of the needs of the particular illnesses or handicaps. Besides personal efforts, the role of close ones, doctors, nursing, psychologists, counsellors etc comes in. Competitors of any type do need peculiar physical and mental abilities to perform better. Animals, like dogs and horses, also could be trained for typical tasks. So, in all categories, shaping of body and mind and keeping them in desired condition involve peculiar exercises. These are united efforts of the individual, the family and the community.

How to exercise is a big question. There are right and wrong sides to it, that is, what is to be done and what is not to be done. While childhood primarily depends on external inputs, most of the youth and adulthood is self-made. Values and lessons received during the childhood are crucial to both mind and body. These remain embedded forever. Right values like honesty, positive thinking, inquisitiveness, focus, tenacity etc could put the mind on a healthy path. Similarly, proper nutrition and fitness routines could keep the body in good shape. If the dominant inputs received inculcate wrong values like cheating, arrogance, carelessness, casualness, negativity etc then the mind treads an unhealthy path. On the same lines, wrong diet, inadequate physical exercise, wrong lifestyle, wrong methods and wrong habits would create health problems to live with. Being the self-governed period, adulthood has a chance to come on the right track, unlearn the wrong values and overcome the physical shortcomings, if any. Such a change, although possible, is often difficult. Wrong childhood habits continue in the later period leading to loss of opportunities. In any case, oldies have only to accept the realities, salvage whatever is feasible, use the wisdom earned to the advantage and remain at peace, relaxed and positive.

There is a general tendency of over-indulgence and straining the body and the mind with unnecessary intakes, inputs and targets. This is nothing but inviting pressure, materially and psychologically. So overfeeding, overdoing and overstraining is a common weakness that overloads the individual with unnecessary fixations and baggage. There is always a rational limit on food intake, physical exercises and work that could be done. Overlooking or taking pride in over-indulgence is nothing but overloading self, often a counterproductive move. It is nothing but creation of personal imbalance that spoils the plot. Anything unnecessary is a waste and strenuous to both body and mind. It is inviting troubles. It needs to be avoided for better performance. I should have done this or should not have done that are typical comments or afterthoughts many individuals spill out in later life. Missing the worthy opportunities due to self-indulgence is a common experience that most live with.

Submitting to or getting trapped in superficial or frivolous ideas is a common weakness. This is a kind of taxing the mind with uncalled for diversions, distortions and aberrations. Diversions like gossips, fantasies, addictions, peer pressures, craze etc. are unnecessarily indulged in, only to dilute the primary focus on the core objective. Distortions occur when predetermined views or ideologies or biases or half-truths or ignorance dominate the thought process. Conclusions and judgements go wrong and the target is missed. Similarly, aberrations set in when actions are based on untruth, misguided inputs, lack of seriousness, communication gaps, unfair motives etc. Taxing the mind with unnecessary stuff is the biggest worry in performing any function. Maintaining the mental focus is a challenge for all. Such training of mind needs serious efforts.

Those who are focused on the job in hand perform better. If the target is set, best path is chosen, time frame is laid, commitment is total and work is in progress, then the performance is bound to be the best. It would be a rewarding experience. Such single minded work culture doesn't get infected with unnecessary and unrelated outside inputs. Invasive addictions get repulsed and the purity of purpose is maintained. Short term gains or instant pleasures are set aside for long term rewards. It is a relaxing situation that keeps the body and the mind in the much desired state. Focus provides the best results.

Mind that knows where to stop, in case of multiple interests, can choose the right path. It is nothing but optimising and balancing the variety of interests. Everything of interest cannot be indulged in. The right way forward is to pick and choose the optimal mix of priority interests. Most persons find it difficult and mess-up the choice. Confusion sets in, focus becomes weak and output misses the target. That is why, best performance remains elusive in most such cases. Balancing is always a big problem and few acquire that art early in life to rise fast. Obviously, outshining examples remain few.

Ultimately, good health and peace of mind is what everyone looks for. Such physical and cognitive capabilities need inputs of right exercise, habits and training to body and mind. Those who succeed in this endeavour would do well not only in performing whatever task undertaken but also in gaining personal satisfaction. Freedom from ailments, purity of thought processes and least personal regrets forms an important feature of their personality. Mostly they are likely to be unassuming and not glamorous. Such exemplary lives is a rarity and worth recognising them for lessons.

Finding Traction to Perform Better

Everyone has some goals. How realistic they are is another issue, but goals do exist. They do help in creating focus. If assessment of the situation is correct, realistic goals are achievable. What all that needs to succeed, if available, there is no reason why goals cannot be reached. The problem is that the assessments often go wrong, situations vary and unknowns prop up on the way. Falling short, unknowns playing mischief and contingency plans not in place, or plans going haywire, could easily spoil the chances of achieving the set goals. Unknowns could also turn out to be an angel/benefactor or luck doing favour and giving unexpected input for success. These may be rare possibilities, but cannot be ruled out. In general, achieving goals is a problem for most. Perhaps over-expectations or under-preparation are the limiting factors.

How to avoid usual blushes of missing the goals is a big question for everybody. How to find right traction to perform better is a permanent challenge to be faced. Depending on the situation one is in, a variety of options are available. Inspiration from within and timely assistance from outside decide the course of action. Multiple options emerge from which one makes a choice, the most ticklish task. The probability of the choice turning out to be right is evenly balanced and eventually the inputs given decide the outcome. Nothing is guaranteed. Some choices create a permanent burden, some are retraceable, some turn out to be benign and some provide good results beyond expectations. It is a mix bag of success and failure. It is worth looking at all that contributes to these outcomes.

Self-motivation is the biggest traction available to every individual. This asset not only looks at the merit of the choice, but also its likely pitfalls. It helps in keeping the contingency plans ready. Such a preparatory exercise not only helps in keeping the situation under control, but also makes midcourse corrections possible. Besides this, the outcome is taken in right spirit and with maturity. No over-excitement in success, no heart-burns in failures, that is the power of self-motivation. Readiness to do the right thing in the given situation is the focus and putting-in the best efforts is the approach. Individuals have achieved great heights through motivated actions in all fields of life including art, music, literature, science, technology, business, sports, media, social work, public service and so on. No shortage of success stories.

Inputs from the near ones is an additional traction that compliments motivation. The help and guidance from family members, friends, well-wishers and conducive public policies provides crucial assistance in moving forward. These timely inputs form a booster to the self-motivated. The enthusiastic support is an inspiration to do better. Timely encouragement, sane advice, financial help, facilitation and professional guidance do help in improving performance. Civilised societies do show this strength of support mechanism. Individual freedom, strong family/civil values, community participation and matured public policies do make a difference in individual performance. It facilitates grooming at the right time, a timely help to nurture talent. Public policies are evolved to create such enabling environment. Identifying talent and nurturing it is attempted both at family level as well as at community level. Parents and teachers do play an important role in these efforts. Essentially it is the culture of the society that creates appropriate base for the individual to rise to the inherent potential.

Developing an insight to identify talent is not an easy task. Raw talent with a potential to be groomed into an achiever is a job cut out for a few. These are mentors who are keen observers of individuals. They are capable of spotting raw talent that is motivated, skilful, receptive and ready to learn. Mentors find it interesting to proceed if the individual is willing to sharpen the raw skills with whatever efforts it demands. Such candidates form a treat for the mentors. They are mutually inspiring and make the job easy. Such combinations are rare examples and also are rare success stories. This is observed in sports, art, music, business, politics, public institutions, social reforms etc. Mentors have groomed achievers in all these fields and there are many examples of exemplary achievements in history. In fact, every big name in history has someone who inspired or guided the achiever to excel.

Professional help is as common as professional rivalries. Professionals sharing tricks of the trade is quite common. In the form of case studies, publications, lectures and interviews many of the insights are put in public domain. There are few secrets and much is free for use. Competition is welcome and also enjoyed. Professional forums/platforms do share information and experiences of mutual benefits. The professional protocols, rules, conventions, needs and studies are shared for collective and individual progress. No one is averse to such exchange for healthy competition. Professional bonhomie is an important traction to progress in professions. However, only knowing a trick is not enough. Its execution and use is a skill that everyone may not possess. Moreover, it is a mind game that few excel in, show personal talent that is often termed as a Gift of God.

Experimentation is common to human nature. So, whatever is available in public domain is tried to be accessed as lessons for adoption. In fact, many problems in one field are tackled by adopting ideas from successes in other fields. Such scouting of parallel cases is quite common. So, ideas developed for physical fitness in one sport come handy for adoption in other sports. Certain physical ailments in various sports are treated with adopted physiotherapy. Teaching methods in science disciplines, such as experimentation, could be adopted effectively in social studies. Methods of discipline and work culture could get adopted from one successful organisation to many other diverse organisations. Instruments developed for research do get adopted for industries, agriculture, health services etc. Progress in technology helps in improving musical instruments, films, graphics, sports and other means of communication and entertainment. So any development in knowledge does not remain restricted to its field of origin. It gets traction for adoption wherever it is found useful. Scouting for new, successful and useful continues in all directions. Utility is a great traction for adoption of new ideas.

Conventional and time-tested methods or available knowledge do not give traction for ever. New ideas have to emerge to meet inadequacies in the existing knowledge. Such Out-of-Box thinking is the biggest asset humans possess. Collectively, trying out something new is the characteristic feature of humans. Building-up knowledge, understand nature and develop useful tools is the special and unique strength of humans. Problems are never left unattended for long. Desire to progress is an added advantage. The combined effect is to attempt new targets and to put the best foot forward. Progress goes on. Trying something new involves risk. But there is no aversion to risk taking. There is a conscious attempt to take risk, individually as also collectively. It is an indication of confidence level to tackle reasonable risks. It is also a sign of innovativeness and entrepreneurship. This mental prowess is the biggest strength of humans. The traction is dormant within and forever ready to be summoned for action. Targets keep rising and there is no stopping. One performs better and inspires others to follow the proven path. The collective wisdom looks for collective good.

Keep Innovating for Progress

Much has been spoken about Innovations in recent times. Progress in computer technology and communication have put innovations on the pedestal as a policy issue. It has also profoundly affected agriculture, industries, banking, management and other sectors of the economy. A close look at this change in the recent past shows a linkage to human nature and human ability to solve existing problems and also look for something new to influence life.

Innovation, a Natural Instinct.

Nature, the physical world around us, does pose problems as it is still not fully understood. So the efforts to understand nature, which signifies development of science and technology, also pose problems to be solved. Human being has the inbuilt natural attitude to solve the problems of nature. This attitude has contributed to development of knowledge, particularly in science and technology and gradually in other areas of human activity. Innovative tools provided by science and technology help other sectors such as agriculture, industry, communication, management, social sciences, art, sports etc. This cumulative build-up of knowledge shows the innovative spirit of human being.

Clearly, innovations have led to progress. Historically, those who adopted innovative practices progressed faster. People moving for trade and commerce, exploration of new lands, development of agricultural tools, use of water, metal work, crafts, leather, ceramics, glass, textiles, medicines, weapons, ships, steam engine, oil, IC engine, electricity, telegraph, automobiles, locomotives, computers, mobiles etc have contributed to progress of people and nations. Those who innovated fast progressed fast. England of 19th century; USA, Germany and Japan of 20th century and perhaps China and India of 21st century are examples of progressive nations. There is a linkage to initiatives for adoption of innovations. Japan was progressing quite well after the Second World War destruction. A study report brought out by UNCTAD around 1970 analysed the progress being made by Japan at that time. The analysis presented showed that the progress was primarily linked to fast absorption of technological and management innovations for industrialization and economic activities. This was further linked to the innovation initiatives and culture built in 18th century Japan during Meiji dynasty. Examples of other progressed nations also indicate similar game changing initiatives.

Innovators are always leaders and get the advantage of the early starters. They remain on a higher pedestal till the followers catch up. If they keep up with the innovative spirit they remain in front. This is true with industries, business and high tech activities. Not innovating with time leads to decline and even collapse as could be seen from the examples of industries in textile, electronics, machinery, printing, computers, mobiles etc.

Innovation is strongly connected to commercialization. It is different from discovery and invention. While discovery is linked to basic scientific principles, invention is a creative step not to the level of commercialization. All inventions do not lead to commercialization. Idea to invention to prototype to final product commercially accepted is a long chain. There are valleys of death between each of these successive steps. For example, only around 2% patents get commercialized. Even after careful selection, only a small percentage of start-ups supported by venture funds succeed and survive. These are realities to be taken seriously.

Development of innovative technology is a very expensive process. It involves method of trial and error, changes and long drawn efforts to come up with a product acceptable to end-user. However, once developed, the product is easy to reproduce or copy as is seen in many consumer durables. Yet one cannot guarantee profit from such ventures. In fact, it is quite difficult to profit from such ventures and even survive. Collapse of ventures is quite common.

Henry Ford, while speaking about success of innovations, has suggested getting answers to basic questions: Is the innovation needed? Is it practical? Is it commercial? There are prominent examples to highlight importance of these questions. Xerox or Photocopying Machine is an interesting example. A lawyer bothered about making copies of petitions to be submitted to court, thought of photocopying the documents and filed the patent. Efforts of over 20 years lead to development of the prototype. Looking at its potential, a paper company took its further development with a motive to raise the market for paper. In the near future the paper company found that production of the photocopying machine itself could be a profitable business. Named the company Xerox and became a multinational and a historical brand name. Velcro is another interesting example. A hiker found a flowery plant material stuck to his socks and needed much effort to remove it. Put under microscope he found it to be small interlocking hooks. Taking help of a weaver he developed the locking tape. The locking tape became a big business in a few years, now well known as Velcro. These examples are revealing for their utility based development and creation of market.

Education: Preparing Minds for Innovations

Education is all pervading activity and invites diverse comments and suggestions from people in different walks of life. Statements from eminent thinkers such as "Education is not just filling a bucket but lighting a fire within" and "Aim of education is not knowledge but action" are indicative of the premise that education is a utilitarian lifelong venture. It is an ability to decipher information for use. It is cognitive strength that is to be built. It is to acquire ability to think. It is the ability to find answers to the questions and problems faced in daily life. This attitude helps in generating ideas and inventive steps. Minds trained to find answers to questions do show promise to be innovative, whichever field they may be associated with. Many eminent personalities have told about the challenges faced by them during childhood and the impact it made on shaping their minds to think of solving problems.

Developing skill in any field needs practice. In case of science and technology, it is the activity based learning or learning by doing is emphasized. This also includes project work. To develop language skill the only method is to read and write. Communication skill or speaking effectively needs practice. Proficiency in social sciences needs project work. Skills in art, music and sports could be developed only by practice. It is the riyaz in music and singing.

Good skills also create base for innovations and creative additions. Even the fields of banking, finance, administration, management, media, communication, defence, sports etc have seen innovative changes. Innovations cover all human activities.

In the middle part of 20th century, Prof. Frederick Terman, at Stanford University, encouraged his engineering students to take the devices and instruments, developed by them in the laboratory, to production level and start manufacturing them. The area provided to them near the university helped the students to start new ventures and become entrepreneurs. Hewlett and Packard were such students and their company HP became a multinational. The area was used by many other students and young entrepreneurs to develop businesses and is now famous as Silicon Valley. Rightfully, Prof. Terman is called the Father of Silicon Valley. The very idea of knowledge institution catalysing young entrepreneurship is a fascinating model to institutionalize innovation. The idea of venture funds also got cultivated in this model. This brought about a big change in economic activities all over during the second half of 20th century. What electricity and IC Engine did in the first half of 20th century, computer technology did in the second half. These are life changing innovations.

Motivation and its nurturing

The natural instinct of innovation need to be summoned and nurtured for progress. This calls for policy initiatives and facilitation in an organised way. This includes greater inputs for research and development, strengthening the regime of Intellectual Property Rights (IPR), encouragement to Venture Funds, support to start-ups, infrastructure development and simplifying regulatory mechanism. There is also a strong need to create facilities for technology incubation, technology packaging and business incubation. These are multidisciplinary needs to start a new venture.

It is a competitive field. Innovations lead to disruptions, call for business restructuring and further innovations. It also leads to failure, particularly for those who do not change. Yet, failure is also a lesson to change. In fact, nothing succeeds like failure. If ventures are failing, then they may not be innovating enough. There must be a freedom to make mistake, otherwise there would be hesitation to try anything new.

To cultivate innovating mind at student level, the concepts of Tod-Phod-Jod and Do-It-Yourself Laboratory need to be promoted. These could encourage creative minds to try new ideas. In fact, idea is the first step in the creative process. It is a long journey from idea to invention to prototype to commercialization and each of these transitions is separated by a valley of death. Only few ideas cross these valleys of death. There is a need to create right kind of support system to cross these valleys. Students need to be encouraged to ask right kind of questions. Only good understanding of the issues can generate right questions. Innovation is also an interdisciplinary effort. Besides various disciplines of science and technology, it needs inputs from economics, finance, management and market. Emerging areas in science and technology need proper infrastructure development. Some of these areas include genetic engineering, medical devices, renewable energy, computing, 3D printing, precision farming, materials etc. Govt needs to create a policy framework to develop these disciplines not only to catch up with others but also try to innovate to be competitive. Greatest failure is to not try.

Innovation is a human activity and if enough of it is not happening then it is a human problem. The hurdle lies in contented inactivity, comfortable inaction, protected laziness and endemic insensitivity that we normally experience. In this respect Quotes from eminent historical personalities are quite revealing. Albert Einstein has said "You cannot solve the problem by the method which in fact created the problem". Economist John Meynard Keynes opined "Problem is not with accepting new ideas but with escaping from the old ones". Innovate, Change and Avoid Beaten Path is the message.

Motivation for Innovation – Raising Pedestal

Aspiration for improvement in quality of life has many facets. Although personal objectives set the tone for individual action, depending on the individual's position in the whole game, there are bound to be social, economic, professional, business and national angles to the way one operates. Situations vary and perceptions differ. Yet the aggregated effect is a certain pattern of development that does favour innovation and change. The society that follows the change aggressively, accepts risks, reforms with strength and takes failures in stride shows faster development.

Growing interdependence in the modern world and growth of variety of services nurtures a broader angle of common interests and societal benefits. Personal benefits within common good have now become a well-accepted approach for development. Depending on the sphere of influence, people do think in terms of sectoral, regional, national and universal benefits. Investments in professional causes and charities, concern towards deprived and weaker sections, growing priority for education and health services, talk of renewable resources and sustainable development, consideration to biodiversity and climate change etc. are significant trends which show broadening of vision of development.

Collective action is quite common in trade, commerce and industries in routine operational matters such as administrative, legal, fiscal, infrastructural and policy issues affecting them. Sectoral associations, chambers and consortia are quite common as pressure groups and lobbies to pursue matters of common interest. However, in case of innovations, collective action is lacking due to narrowed perceptions about individual initiatives, personal benefits and the uncertainties involved in possible gains.

Entrepreneurship is an unpredictable and unique attribute, difficult to define clearly and much difficult to identify. Consideration of intellectual property rights, commercial potential of innovation, desire of secrecy for exclusive personal benefits and investments/efforts gone into creative achievements put limitations on making innovation a common task. It continues to remain individualised operation. Subcritical and marginal sphere of influence of the individual innovators is a limiting factor in generating combined action. Yet the recent trends in encouragements to start-ups, evolving venture funding, angel funding, crowd funding, incubation facilities and growing urge to innovate is a welcome change taking place all over.

The performance of associations and consortia in different sectors in developed countries are qualitatively different than those in the developing countries due to the sphere of influence, levels of skills, nature of markets and overall capabilities and aspirations for innovations. The process, efforts and infrastructure in the developed countries are better organised showing progress through innovations as a bigger common agenda. Developing world is still to mature to play any significant role in this process. It is still in a learning mode. Naturally there is no global consensus on competitive development objectives linked to innovation. In essence, differences in global view are linked to the share in the global market, strength of the economy, enormity of the internal challenges and level of self-confidence in the competitive environment. Global economy is still in the transition phase and trying to adjust to new realities of interdependence, limitations on resources, climate change and new standards.

The lack of innovation culture is more endemic in the developing world. Research and Development is still either routine, fashionable or peripheral. It is not taken seriously as a means to become competitive. Resource constraints and manpower shortage makes it still more difficult to try something new and invest in scientific research. This lack of seriousness in R&D initiative is also reflected in lack of seriousness in dealing with issues related to IPR, commercializing innovations and transfer of technology. In countries with large internal market, it is a dampening factor to achieve higher exports in a competitive regime. Import of technology is often seen as an easy option. When easier options are available there is a poor motivation to innovate and compete. When there is not much to lose or the very survival is not under threat, inaction continues.

In the absence of a common cause for the innovators, it is imperative that the country has to find a policy option that can catalyse and motivate common action by all concerned. In some of the developing countries like India, consensus is gradually building up on strategic initiative for innovation and technology transfer as a national policy. Innovation has still not grown into a visible movement that could eventually become a well-accepted culture. Issues are getting articulated and policies are getting evolved, but assimilating innovation mechanism takes time. Much needs to be done and the efforts/programmes have to be long term, participatory and sustainable.

Reaching a higher pedestal to compete in the global setting and match the strength of the frontrunners is a stupendous task. It needs strategic approach, adequate inputs and sustained efforts commensurate with the requirement. Perceptions have to mature to accept competition and innovations as a way of life. It is a challenge to achieve competitive development. To provide core strength to this process, priority needs to be given to education and health services. Overall literacy status has to rise substantially to build ambition in the society and release the dormant talent for research and innovation. Well-informed, educated and healthy population is a key to development through innovative spirit and entrepreneurship.

Raising the pedestal through supportive public policies and resource inputs could generate motivation for innovation in the people. The desired ecosystem needs not only strong research and development facility, but also skilled researchers, demanding stakeholders from various professions/sectors raising right problems to work on and active venture funds to select inventions for commercialisation. The intermediate steps of product design, prototyping, market testing and productionising on a sound economic basis calls for much hard work and sound judgements on final products. Technological innovations are driving innovations in other sectors like human resource development, finance, transport, communication, health, business and management. The change is visible. Such an ecosystem is a dream setting, a raised pedestal to be experienced and lived with for success stories. It is a vision to be transmitted to those lagging behind, action to be inspired and process to be established. It needs highly credible leadership to make it a reality, a rare asset.

Creative instinct, inventive step, potential utility, user needs, user demand, techno-economic viability of the idea and passion to deliver are essential attributes to innovate successfully. Entrepreneurship is at the core of innovation. The risk is immense, but the outcome could be exciting. Entrepreneur needs that pedestal and support to succeed. Such motivation needs the right environment. Society needs to provide that to develop.

Impulse for Creativity

Creativity is a dormant potential everyone possesses. It is ready to be summoned, but needs a situation for impulse. What gives impulse to creative thinking? Broadly, every human action is a response to a given situation. Chivalry, kindness, anger, humour, joy, cooperation, creativity etc are hidden human attributes which get outlet only in conducive situations, a kind of impulse to act. For example, a success brings joy, failure generates sympathy, sacrifice give rise to regards, odd behaviour leads to humour, irritation creates anger, common interests boost cooperation and deprivation gives impulse to kindness. Creativity is no different. It needs a challenge, a problem and inspiration to work to find a solution or invent something new. If individual has the background to deal with the problem, the action emerges. All creative actions may not succeed, but the attempt is prompted with hopes. Multiple problems, challenges and observations lead to multiple potential solutions and options to attempt. Choice is left to the aspirational individual.

Difficulties is a common experience throughout the lifespan. These could be personal as well as common; related to profession, health, finance, family and community; linked to unknowns, ignorance, logistics and choices; arising out of accidents, natural disasters or circumstances and so on. So, responding to the difficulties and challenges is what everyone does day-in and day-out. Nature and level of difficulties, personal capabilities and available support system decide the future course of action. Creative mind-set or problem solving attitude plays a big role in overcoming the difficulties. Essentially, creativity is a search for realistic and feasible options to proceed with.

Creativity is also an outlet for supressed emotions. Inner desire to try something new, experimental and tangible do exist in everyone. Finding opportunity to experience what is in mind is not always possible. Till the opportune time, these desires remain bottled in mind. Rarity of such opportunity is the real limitation. People keep trying to their limit. Some succeed, some do not. The creative instincts remain dormant in most cases, leaving behind only memories of attempts made, or not made, and unfulfilled dreams. People do speak about such things and express regrets for not being able to demonstrate their creativity or missing the chances or not getting the right opportunity. Such emotional reflections are quite common, with a rider of acceptance of inevitability.

Often, people do get stuck in wrong situations. To come out of these, they do stretch their imagination. This reaction tries all possible creative options. It is a feverish try to cross the barrier. Where opportunities are limited, this becomes an uphill task. One gets badly stuck and have to adjust with the fate accompli. This happens with careers, professions, family, social life, health and so on. Creative minds have a better chance to find a way out. So changing careers, professions, locations, lifestyles etc have been successfully tried by those who have shown creativity, taken risks and perceived doggedly to the finish. Of course, overall this is a rarity. Those who try seriously may find a way out.

Looking at the problem in multiple angles may provide a clue to find a way out. Such diverse thinking to evaluate the situation and to explore new ideas, options, avenues, escapes, compromises etc could throw up feasible solution. This is kind of opening up the mind for new thoughts and new inputs for finding out-of-box solutions to the problem. Obviously it is a search for creative path. It could be tackling the problem head-on, or skirting it or find a compromise. The problem is to be solved on feasibility criteria. Ultimately it has to be a workable solution. Creativity has a realistic and practical angle and not just a flight of imagination that goes nowhere.

In a way, creativity is a complex chemistry of curiosity, reflectivity, individuality, questioning, contemplative and certainly disruptive. That is why it is a slow process and not a planned outcome with standard operating procedure. The churning involved is unknown, and outcome is also unknown. Inventions, discoveries, new art forms, new techniques, new tools etc are all evolved creations with diverse inputs from diverse sources over a long period of time. It is a cumulative build-up with contributions from multiple individuals and sources. New creations may be assigned to some individuals, but it is a known fact that it is a culmination of a series of silent contributions in the past.

Those with high conventional IQ are not necessarily creative. In fact, they are most likely to be logical, orderly and efficient smooth sailors. These highly structured minds are focused and are unlikely to be prone to diverse thinking, a slow process that looks for unknowns, uncharted and is by far unstructured. Any focused thinking individual, well programmed, with robotic efficiency, primarily non-disruptive, is like a well-oiled machine that functions smoothly and delivers fast. These individuals are slotted to perform efficiently in doing what is conventional and well charted. Any deviation is not expected to find easy acceptance. Speed is their strength. Curious, searching, struggling, persuasive and reflective methods are anathema to them. Slow evolving creativity is not their cup of tea and doesn't find attraction for them.

Creativity often finds an outlet when one reaches a dead end, pushed against the wall, reach the ceiling, a breaking point or an upper limit. For example, a challenge for survival makes one aggressive and willing to do anything risky and challenging. This may bring a turning point where changing course is the only option. For example, career stagnations are overcome by job hopping or shifting to a different profession. Bankruptcies are tackled by feasible restructuring and rehabilitation. Business stagnations are handled by innovations and diversifications. In a way, reaching a dead end gives impulse to find a new venture, a new beginning and a new creative try.

Challenge of any form becomes a starting point for creative thinking. Good going brings relaxation. If things are not normal, then something new has to be tried. One starts looking for an out-of-box solution. This needs lateral thinking, search for ideas and willingness to try something new. In fact, creativity is not a choice to begin with. Facing difficulties and challenges in normal working makes one to think laterally. A cosy situation does not bring motivation for lateral thinking and creativity. Lives of creative individuals do reveal high level of agitation, disturbance and dislocations. They had to come out of the situation and struggle and try something new, a creative outcome. Path of outstanding creations is too tough and risky. No one accepts it as a first choice. Motivation comes from impulse of challenges and the disquiet about the situation one is in. Passions are high, will is alive, attempts are being made, but the situation is not in favour. The trail left behind become an input for someone else to make use of for success in future. Eventually, cumulative creative attempts do succeed in giving a visible and useful output.

Shield of Afterthoughts

Imaginations, expectations and predictions going wrong is not uncommon. In fact, everyone faces such embarrassment, quite often. Such events are either self-created, influenced by many unknowns, chance happenings, others playing a role, or simply outcome of personal shortcomings. How to overcome these embarrassments is a real question. Face it head-on, try to cover it up, downplay it or simply ignore it. This hints at the nature of a person. Honest, bold, combative, timid, jingoist, hard nut, histrionic, manipulative and twister are some of the characteristics seen in individuals. Which one prevails in an embarrassing situation is anybody's guess.

Individuals like to take credit wherever there is a success story. I had said it so, I had guessed it correctly, I had advised so, I had contributed to make it work, I was a torchbearer of the idea/mission/task, I lead it from the front etc are some of the credit grabbing statements. A small role played is disproportionately blown up. This happens with those who are in a vintage situation or a power position. If it is a failure, obvious reaction is to distance oneself from the story or if that fails, then attempt to cover-up. In such cases, the common response is, I don't know, I wasn't there, I have nothing to do with it, I was misguided, it was a overlook, it is a minor thing etc are some of the responses to downplay the matter. The other strategy could be to point out others' failures in justification, divert attention towards other issues or resort to counterattack to come out of the mess. These are motivated responses for rationalization and to cover-up personal shortcomings. These are afterthoughts, used as shield.

Embarrassing situations arise primarily out of ignorance. Ill-informed would resort to wild guesses which often go wrong. On the other hand, predictions and expectations based on knowledge and rigour have a better chance of being closer to the truth. Studies, experiments, experience and well established protocols have become the basis for predictions, and proceed with, to achieve the desired objective. That is the sign of knowledge driven modern society. No project or service delivery could succeed on wild guesses. That would only bring embarrassment. Expanding knowledge and specialisations are in a way reducing the possibilities of embarrassments even in more complex professional services, such as organ transplants, and missions, like space missions. In this, even failures do not bring embarrassment and, in fact, encourage renewed efforts. No cover-up is tried and hurdles are crossed.

Creation of aura or false image is another source of embarrassment. Image building is often resorted to for improving chances in competitive arena. To achieve power, get recognition, impress others and push for personal interests or simply to remain in limelight, some do try to improve self-image. This may include projecting attributes like being honest, humble, tough, strong, humane, smart, skilful etc, much sought after images in public eye. These could also be used as camouflage to hide weaknesses and dubious intensions. Such deliberate attempt to package persona may not always work. If it is a false image, it may get exposed sooner than later. If the reality or the truth comes out, the embarrassment is a certain outcome. Overplaying with false images increase the possibility of over-exposure, often creating awkward situations. Of course, some may be thick-skinned enough to live with the outcome and the embarrassment.

Some show early promise. Rankers, smart ones, early starters, well placed, well connected etc do get an early break and raise expectations. Many of them missing the way in due course is quite common. Losing the steam due to loss of motivation, wrong choices, lack of stamina, diversions, overexposure, buckling under pressures etc is a common experience. This falling short of expectations is witnessed in all fields of activity. In fact, over-expectations, like in professions, is a menace for many. It only creates unnecessary pressure that diminishes the focus that is so very essential for good performance. On the other hand, those who show less promise but have tenacity, focus, relaxed demeanour and persuasive attitude may perform better than expected. These are unassuming characters who rise from nowhere and over-perform. Creative individuals, dogged performers, silent workers, skilful operators eventually do better in whatever activity they have chosen. If expectations and glamour are dissociated, falling short could be avoided.

In professional and competitive activity, falling short of expectations is normally taken sportively. Rules of the game are in place and evolved to be fair to all. However, in social and political arena there is much subjectivity, complexity and wide grey area to act. Failures are tried to be explained to reduce embarrassment. Combative posturing is often resorted to for salvaging the situation. It is usually a blame game. Counter attack is another method, attractive way for defending failures. In this, the other side is blamed as having resorted to malpractices or unethical means. Allegations are used as a strategic tool. The free for all accusations is peculiar to day-to-day social life, dominated by gossips and wild chatter, where proving is nobody's responsibility. This is typical looseness that prevails in variety of social conflicts and political arena. Tit-for-tat is the line of thinking and accepting mistakes or shortcomings is not taken as wisdom of common interests. Personal interests and narrow posturing are kept above the common interests. Greater prevalence of such positioning remains a serious matter and a source of embarrassment.

Falling short of expectations is often not a personal failure. It is most likely to be a combination of parameters, many of them extraneous, beyond anticipation and not within one's control. So, if enough efforts have been put in, why one should take failure as a source of embarrassment. Courage of conviction should accept it as a fair outcome and a reality to be tackled dispassionately. Taking it to heart is unnecessary as it indicates an element of diffidence. Continue with renewed efforts is a correct approach. This element of courage is the positive thinking to move on. Every try for crossing a hurdle, and not stopping to try, is the way forward and possibly a path to eventual success.

Keeping higher expectations as a source of motivation could be a conscious strategy. It would be based on understanding of strengths and limitations. Any result would be taken sportively. The problem arises when expectations are based on inadequate groundwork, ignorance and dreamy approach. Ego and false pride also boost expectations. In this approach, there are no regrets for shortcomings and no introspection for rectification. This is invitation for failure. The result is blame games and finding scapegoats. Such hard nuts and frozen minds look for justifications and negative escape routes. These afterthoughts are for finding cover to hide. It is nothing but a desperate attempt to shield oneself from embarrassment. Best path is to be realistic in expectations and accepting realities in right spirit. It is the best shield to avoid embarrassment. In that case, there is no need of afterthoughts for covering up, and no further embarrassments. Avoiding escapist shield of afterthoughts and focusing on preparedness would be more rewarding and relaxing. Prevention is better than cure.

Skill, Knowledge and Action

Understanding a topic, its contents and its potential applications is knowledge based. In fact, action emanates from knowledge. It is the theoretical foundation that justifies action. This action is the practice or practical use of the theory. Yet, one who knows theory better may not be able to practice it effectively and vice a versa. Those who can do both would be a rare combination. This is true in all fields of activity. In a way, most actions are driven by common sense, motivation, likes/dislikes and needs. So, any action of a child could be linked to needs or action of a teenager could be linked to likes and dislikes. Such impulsive behaviours are common with adults also. Individuals keep struggling to respond to a situation as unknowns overwhelm knowns. Process of learning is endless, unknowns plenty and, in reality, actions are never fool-proof. Human being continues to be inherently and broadly ignorant.

Management expert who is theoretically sound is often not a businessman. On the other hand, a successful businessman is normally not a management expert as is perceived to be. In fact, the term entrepreneurship indicates something wider than business and expertise, as normally taken to be. Entrepreneur cannot be put in narrow slot of persons running ongoing business and those giving informed advice. Entrepreneurship indicates passion to create wealth, take risks, gauge market opportunities, manage people, mobilise resources, solve problems, innovate and so on. This is particularly true of first generation entrepreneurs. The recent surge in technology driven entrepreneurship has brought the concept of start-ups in prominence. Special incentives in the form of funding and policy support, growth of venture and angel funding, infrastructure growth, rise in demand for variety of services and inclination towards self-employment has brought good days for entrepreneurship. They are well informed passionate businessmen, not necessarily management experts.

Political decisions on national economy are not taken by economists. Leadership arising out of political process is responsible for decisions, including economic decisions. This is linked to national choice of political leadership, a combined opinion on a bunch of issues covering social, economic and ideological aspects influencing the thinking at a given point of time. So, economic decisions need not be based on economic theories alone. Variances and compromises are the domain of the political leadership. Executive actions are a choice of leadership, not of experts. By the way, experts themselves could hold opposing views. Leadership can make a choice of its liking, well fitted into its thinking. Diversity of expert opinions itself is a safety net for the leadership to follow its own path. Use experts to do whatever you wish and, as intellectuals, leave them fighting/arguing in perpetuity. That is the beauty of the political structure that is built on inherent human diversity. A political scientist may be able to analyse a political event, but he is unlikely to be an active participant in the event. Post event analysis is more of a theoretical exercise to unfold the multiple facets of the event, good for posterity. Politician, however, participates in generating the event. Similar is the case with the ideologues who have influence in political process, deciding the agenda and influencing the political executive in decision making. Yet the political leadership has to take a final call with political judgement. Economists, political scientists, ideologues or any other experts have a limited role of giving inputs to the political leadership for taking decisions.

In literary creations, a writer does the original work in the form of novel, play, poetry, stories, scripts etc. These creations are inspirational in nature and unique to the writer. So we see the variety in such creations linked to social and economic conditions, human nature and conflicts, situational influence, interaction with nature, adventures and so on. Human imagination and perceptions have ample scope to create a theme that could be attractive to others. Similar creative outputs are also seen in respect of paintings, sculptures, crafts, music, architecture, films, cartoons, photography etc. These artists look for beauty, impressions, reality, novelty etc in their creations and these are admired by others. Critics is another category that is much knowledgeable and insightful to comment on creations. Critics are not creators, but do help in understanding the strengths and weaknesses in the creations. They look at the variety of creations dispassionately and are good at comparative analysis to provide a balanced picture. Their comments are useful to art lovers and common people to understand the creations. Art appreciation is a subjective method and varies with the individual. It has limited scope for quantification. Commercial success of a work of art is difficult to gauge. In fact, some of the works have become commercially successful after the death of the artist. Such examples have drawn much attention of academicians and critics as a topic of research. Artistic creativity is a subtle and mischievous subject loaded with diverse opinions, glamorous yet brutal outcome, unpredictable returns, odd and clumsy behaviour of artist, individualistic, opinionated and devoid of rational logic.

Monetary gains to critics and analysts are likely to be stable and better, unlike to artists, an inbuilt paradox.

In case of sports, situation is slightly different. Player has to perform, use personal skill and show results. To improve this performance and give better results, the sportsperson has to hone the skills, reduce the shortcomings and adopt sustainable protocols to be better prepared. This job is done by the coach who understands the game, judge the sportsperson properly and provide the guidance needed. The coach may or may not be a sportsman himself, but he may have a better eye to judge the sportsperson to suggest corrective measures. So the role of a coach is of a theoretician observing and guiding the player to improve the performance. Based on these inputs, the player executes the task. In the highly competitive games, coach plays a crucial role and the player is much dependant on him or her. Coach or trainer does make a difference in the output of a player.

Another interesting area of theory versus practise is that of invention and innovation. A new product or process is an inventive step, establishing a new use of science or technology. Such invention is a new method or a principle of doing a job. However, innovation is a step where the invention could be put to use, commercialized. The economic sustainability of a marketable product converts invention into innovation. Broadly, one can say that inventor is a theoretician while innovator is a practitioner. Every invention cannot become an innovation. There are valleys of death between the two. Commercial success is a rare thing. That is why innovators is a rare breed.

In the realm of human behaviour, we see people passing judgements on diverse subjects without a pause. It could be anything concerned with our daily life, such as social issues, politics, sports, education, entertainment, people, jobs, finance etc on which everyone has an opinion to give. One may know very little about the subject matter, but that does not deter one from giving a judgemental opinion. Developing understanding before giving an opinion is never considered as a prerequisite. Views based on scanty information is more of a gossip than well-formed opinion. To be judgemental in itself is dangerous, more so in a gossip format. It is practice without theory, an antithesis of scientific or logical thinking. Greater prevalence of gossip is a sign of underdevelopment or backwardness. Better to come out of it. Surely, the creative, gifted, unique and influential acts do not fall in the category of gossip. Such exceptional contributions deserve admiration without hesitation.

Understanding Knowledge

Knowledge, as understood by humans, cannot grow in isolation. It needs purpose and the purpose clearly is to improve living conditions. In the modern society, pursuit of knowledge has a strong economic angle linked to all aspects of human welfare. Knowledge is an economic good helping in improving the quality of life. Wealth creation, job creation, adding variety of activities, enhancing capabilities, looking beyond survival etc are manifestations of knowledge. Rapid growth in knowledge is clearly visible in all disciplines, a cumulative build-up. New ideas, new tools, new resources, new activities, new aspirations are all getting added continuously, creating new avenues to work on. Improvisations lead to obsolescence and adoption of new knowledge becomes necessary. Recognition of this reality makes economic sense. Change with new knowledge is the need.

Knowledge growth is particularly rapid in science and technology. This not only influences economic growth but also provides new tools to other disciplines such as industry, agriculture, energy, habitat, communication, economics, politics, management, social sciences, art, etc. Science and technology becomes central to existing as also new disciplines. For example, origin and growth of space technology and information technology is directly linked to growth of knowledge base in science and technology. Agriculture, health, food, transport and other existing sectors are all influenced by core disciplines of science and technology. Art, sports and communications are getting new tools to innovate and further evolve. Strength in basics is a key factor in knowledge expansion.

Capacity to produce and utilize new knowledge forms the core of competitive progress. Those who have recognised this reality and work on it have improved living conditions. Improvements in manpower, skills and infrastructure, besides focus on well set targets, give clear edge in performance and capacity building. Creation of knowledge is an ongoing process, universal and participatory in nature, mutually dependant, open ended and forms a public asset. Knowledge is shared, debated, published, used, updated and mostly remains in public domain. Monopolistic, secretive, distributive, specialized, partial etc are attributes associated with knowledge depending on the situation. What is known is incomplete, subject to change and has to be taken with a pinch of salt.

Knowledge is more than information. While information is a structured data, which is passive and inert, knowledge indicates cognitive capability. Knowledge is a capacity to decipher information to give it a meaning and develop understanding of the basic contents. In a way, when information is set aside, what remains is knowledge. Language does put limits on knowledge in the sense that known words may be inadequate to explain everything that is understood. We can know more than what we can explain. Inadequacy of existing vocabulary to explain what is understood is a common experience. Besides codified knowledge, which is adequately articulated, there also exists uncodified or tacit knowledge which has a greater feel of the underlying processes those cannot be adequately explained in words. We often hear the terms like gut feeling, hunch, nuance, judgement etc which project the subjective, qualitative or holistic understanding of the subject or issue or situation under consideration. Language inadequacy is experienced, quite often, by everyone.

Acquisition of knowledge is a lifelong and unending exercise. Education may provide methodological training and skilling to acquire knowledge. Yet the real learning depends on using information, devices and products, or doing things oneself. Activity based learning, learning by doing, is often emphasized to develop cognitive capability and skill. Similarly, experience is valued for the insight that it develops. Real life problems are better tackled by experience and interaction.

Knowledge is available to all and does not decline by distribution. Knowledge could remain dormant and may revive with need of the time. Knowledge is not absolute, and varies with new inputs, situations and needs. It is a work in progress. Knowledge helps to generate new knowledge, cannot be overgrazed to be lost forever. Value of knowledge is in its use for the benefit of all. Knowledge build-up in a variety of activities has helped in improving the quality of life. Accumulation of knowledge in agriculture, nutrition, health, energy, habitat, transport, communication etc over time has shown visible change in human life. From aboriginal to modern human is a big change. When looked at in a disaggregated form, knowledge is useful to some, useless to some and mysterious to some. So, mathematics may be useful to a computer programmer, but alien to a singer. Physics may be useful to a nuclear engineer, but useless to an orthopaedic surgeon. Motivation to acquire knowledge is generally limited to personal needs linked to overall survival. Few do keep a broad objective of contributing to societal benefits or simply to satisfy creative passion. Accumulation of knowledge is a combined effect of all these efforts.

New, improved and useful developments are accepted fast. New areas of research and studies are taken up as a challenge. Those ambitious try to acquire higher skills. New knowledge sticks well with ambitious and motivated. They do contribute to further developments in their chosen areas. However, the isolated contributions in different disciplines remain unused, in silos. Integrating these fragmented elements of wider knowledge base and converting it into utilitarian packages of benefit to people is a big challenge. Science, technology, economics, social sciences and their sub-disciplines in isolation cannot deliver anything. Coming together of these elements of knowledge, in right proportions, can deliver something useful and acceptable to the ultimate users. This is a felt need, but far from being met. Can this process of integration get accentuated? Pressure is getting built up to come out of silos. It is time to respond positively and show tangible benefits to the people. The recent trend towards interdisciplinary and multi-disciplinary work culture is encouraging and could meet the needs of the people.

Knowledge is a capital freely available to the potential users. As consumers of goods and services, this knowledge is used by the people, knowingly and unknowingly. So a user of mobile telephone need not know the technological details, but acquires only user skills. Similarly, electric gadgets, medical devices, transport, processed food, clothing, shelter etc are knowledge driven items put to use by people without knowledge. Such user friendly devices and products need investments and form the consumption capital. Producers of these devices get inputs from scientists, technologists, economists, social scientists, management experts etc and try to meet the consumer needs. The effected investment is the production capital. All this put together involves knowledge investment. In a way knowledge is a capital that completes the chain of production and consumption. Multidisciplinary knowledge base is linked to human needs, human aspirations and desire to learn and add to the knowledge. The process continues unabated. Knowledge is a means to an end, to improve quality of life. Who can ignore this hard earned treasure?

Case of Tacit Knowledge

Much has been said about knowledge, though missing the conceptual clarity. Repository of information, formatted or structured information of subjects, special skills in disciplines or domain expertise, practising ability, language or articulation skill etc are related elements of the knowledge base in a broad sense. Deciphering information is the ability to understand the contents in the information that enables to put it to use and also add to it. This ability could be broadly termed as knowledge. Information may keep varying, but the ability to understand it is the brain power built over time. Knowledge is a time varying asset.

Information keeps generating and flowing, but the knowledge development is linked to individual's attitude towards information. There is a learning process and a good learner could acquire the relevant insight. Take the case of experience. It is a rich source of knowledge. Keen observer of events, learning by doing, participation in action and sharing of experience are effective methods of building up knowledge. This sticks well and an open mind can get right inputs from experiencing. Taking the right lessons from the experience is individual's capability to build knowledge.

While formal inputs are received during education and on the job activities and training, there are variety of informal inputs received at home, from the neighbourhood, from the social interactions, from media and random events happening around. Normal inquisitiveness in a person can gather many lessons from these inputs. Forming opinions is individual's choice, but inputs received are generally benign and neutral. A positive mind and sincere efforts to understand nature's secrets and processes can bring right wisdom to individual. Such a knowledge base inspires to undertake creative and useful activities.

Diverse information essentially helps in building up nuances, the ability to understand the underlying processes in nature and human behaviour. Why a particular event or action or reaction happens could be best understood with right nuances, intuitions, hunches or common sense. That is tacit knowledge. Such subjective analysis becomes essential in unbiased relative assessments, particularly in grey areas of happenings around, loaded with many unknowns. Information about nature is limited and human behaviour is fragile, leaving no option but to grope in the dark. The search for truth is an uphill task. It is an unending game that human being keeps playing with the help of both structured and tacit knowledge. It is a test of one's intellect, inquisitiveness and tenacity.

When known information is kept aside, what remains is knowledge, the ability that gives meaning to the information. The nuances built, if unbiased, have the best chance to make fair judgements on the happenings around. Such unbiased views are likely to be closest to the truth, although not the complete truth. Fairness in judgements needs to be the basic objective in any endeavour. That is the surest way to progress, a kind of channelization of efforts. That is why much emphasis is put on playing by rules, ethics in business, fairness in competition, merit based choice, assigning task linked to capability, competence in performance, equality of opportunity, openness in dealings etc. Preambles, core principles and mission statements in any task essentially articulate this approach. Any dilution in this would show the adverse consequences, which we often experience in real life situations. Drifting from fairness and rules is a sure path to aberrations and even chaos.

For ages, comprehension has been a part of formal method of teaching languages. It seeks to develop ability to summarise the theme or core point of a given text. It is considered as an important test of gauging the level of understanding. Any story or a topic or an episode could be told in brief, if understood correctly. It helps in drawing reasonable conclusions, a need in daily life. Often one faces situations which need fair assessment to proceed. Ability to comprehend and identify core issues comes handy to decide the focus and the further course of action. Such wisdom is what one looks for to act confidently, bear with whatever outcome and be at peace as the action was well thought out.

Just as comprehension is important, a deeper understanding of a subject is equally important. Such insight is a sign of having a feel of the details, pros and cons, much needed for fair judgement. An expert in a subject is supposed to have such insight and disaggregated picture of the situation to be dealt with. In specialized fields such as science, engineering, medicine, agriculture, environment etc expertise is developed with objectivity and much rigour. That is why expert opinions become vital in crucial decisions of big consequences and long term impact.

In all the knowledge linked actions, the focus needs to be on understanding the reality or on search for truth. Only impartial outlook can make this possible. Truth has no bias and its search is a noble and desirable task. Predetermined views may miss the passage to truth. Positive and open minded individuals have the best chance of reaching the truth. Sweet or bitter, truth demands its complete acceptance. It could be tackled appropriately. Vitiating or ignoring the truth would be detrimental in the long run. It does not spare anyone. Acceptance of truth provides the right chance to rectify the situation.

Natural processes are full of unknowns. Fair questioning and sceptical approach could bring essential rigour in finding the truth. Nothing should be taken on face value and checked from all possible angles. This is of particular importance in case of actions having wider ramifications. For example, big economic development initiatives, such as mega infrastructure or industrial projects, may have unknown health and environmental ramifications those cannot be ignored. Issues like climate change, spread of viruses, lifestyle diseases, conservation of biodiversity, treating toxic wastes, impact of artificial intelligence etc are posing new challenges. Impact of technology on learning skills and human behaviour do need a careful look. As not fully known, Nature's dynamics need serious consideration.

Finding the causes of new problems is one aspect, but yearning to know more about Nature is inbuilt in human psyche. Cumulative built up of knowledge is out of human ambition, adventure, endemic inquisitiveness and curiosity about all that exists around. Whether it is massive galaxy or microscopic bacteria, human being wants to know whatever exists in the universe. Knowing more and more and going deeper and deeper is the desire. Improving life is in mind and developing useful knowledge is the work in progress. Developing deeper understanding is the desire. This uncodified and immeasurable insight or tacit knowledge about the man-made tools and methodologies provide the enabling means to act and reach the goal. Human hunger for progress remains. No stopping of this human adventure to know more. In this, non-transferable tacit knowledge that is individual centric plays a significant role along with the codified knowledge available in open domain. Ultimately, with individual, the tacit knowledge also goes in oblivion. Secrets of individual mind remain secrets forever. Individual's insights and skill are never fully known. Tacit knowledge is individual's possession.

Survival vs Knowledge Seeking

Like any other animal, the basic instinct of any human is that of survival. If survival is assured, then other things follow. This may include education, recreation, career, family, community etc. Seeking knowledge is something that is high end expectation, a rare possibility. Creativity, innovation, research, adventure, exploration etc are knowledge focused activities very few venture into. Such aspirations call for passion, taking risk, much efforts and perseverance. Obviously, such knowledge seekers or talent is not common.

Primacy of survival is understandable. But, unlike animals, humans can go beyond survival. The thinking faculty makes it possible to look for beyond survival. Ability to understand the surrounding nature, intervene in it and try for change is unique to humans. Activity is not confined to food alone, but looks to know more, develop tools, put them to use and search for new avenues for progress and happiness. So besides survival, humans evolved and added housing, clothing, medicines, agriculture, industry, education, cultural outlets, services and so on. These were need-based, aspirational and knowledge driven developments. More and more ideas and activities got added over centuries and millennia. Small number of knowledge seekers and innovators kept adding to these activities of benefit to all. That is why they are revered by all.

Yet most individuals do keep modest expectations of survival and be at peace. The struggle involved in survival itself is stiff enough for most and scope for anything beyond this is limited.

Vast majority is more focused on day-to-day living. Live a peaceful life gets primacy. Only passionate knowledge seekers try to go beyond survival and struggle for it. The idea of enjoying life itself is restricted to few recreational methods of mental relaxations and material consumption. Why bother about the mentally and physically taxing ways of life like study, honing skills, practicing and innovating. Work for simple survival remains a struggle for most. Options for anything more are limited. Modest expectations arise out of struggle involved in pursuing attractive and competitive avenues of work. Most accept this reality, feel that they are not cut out for something ambitious and keep a modest objective. Knowledge seeking, except for that needed for day-to-day needs, is beyond their consideration. Working class doing structured routine tasks falls in this category. It is struggling with normal routines and unwilling to look beyond, may be out of circumstances.

Monotonous work and no significant change makes life boring and leads to fatigue. How to enjoy the day-to-day life remains the main concern for this class. There are a few common sources of enjoyment. The first focus is on food. Most like to be foody within the limits of affordability. Trying different recipes, visits to restaurants/outlets of choice, finding occasions for feasting, joining festivities, touring for food indulgence etc are methods adopted to enjoy food. Next source of enjoyment is entertainment. Music, sports, video programmes, reading material, socialising, tours, family gatherings etc are common sources of enjoyment for most. These outlets keep one informed and provide necessary relaxation. For some, getting carried away by addictions is also enjoyment.

Drinking and smoking are common addictions which beyond a limit could be damaging. In a way, individuals struggle to find their palatable path within the modest expectations.

There are few who do have long term thinking, ambition and bigger vision. They are learners and look for knowledge within their field of activity and also beyond. They enjoy looking for new, unknown and contribute to their activity. Some are inquisitive, innovative and have creative instinct. They not only acquire knowledge, but contribute to existing knowledge with in-built creativity. This enrichment of knowledge remains forever and benefits everyone. Knowledge seeking is a spiritual journey. It is a selfless contribution. This spirituality is a search for truth. It needs dedication and struggle, attributes very few endowed with, and perform. It is a contribution for the better future. Knowledge creation has remained a job for a few. Future is in their mind and present action is aimed at that goal.

Some have an urge to understand nature. Surrounding fascinates them and motivates them to reveal the secrets of things around. This includes humans, animals, plants, objects, climate etc. Behaviour of humans and animals, existence of plants and their diversity, forms of objects and their characteristics, their interdependence etc are subjects of curiosity for many. These are naturally existing things and have influence on each other. Understanding these mutual interactions and interdependence is a fascinating subject of art, literature and science. It is an open field for creativity and adding to knowledge. Inspiring ideas emanate from these nature's bounties. This cumulative built-up of knowledge makes life meaningful and enjoyable. Nature is a source of survival and progress. Biodiversity makes it a beautiful world to live and let live. It is a source of inspiration to move on.

If survival is assured, why not try something new? Some do try new ideas, create something novel, innovate, explore, adventure etc for self-satisfaction. This needs passion to know more and do more. It could be for knowledge contribution, for economic value, for social causes or for personal ambition. In a way, it is for personal pleasure and satisfaction. It calls for motivation and commitment for useful output. Motivation arises out of personal liking, impulse from someone, experiencing exciting events, impact making observations, tragedies, jubilations, successes, failures, revelations about personal potential and so on. Motivation is individual centric and does not apply to all uniformly. Stories of motivated individuals are unique and often inspiring. Motivation creates ambition to prove something new and satisfying. Big achievers in any field are motivated to prove something of their choice. Their success proves their passion. The in-built talent finds an outlet in unique situation, specific to the person. It is a unique combination of passion, motivation, ambition and circumstances. Not possible for everyone.

Finding traction for achieving higher goals is a rarity. A large majority is stuck with survival instinct and modest expectations. Rising in the ladder of higher and higher goals keeps getting difficult. The pyramidal structure of achievers is obvious, clearly discernible and universally accepted. People do admire and respect achievers. Unique achievements are celebrated. So we find icons, leaders and celebrities in all fields of activities. Creativity, skill and knowledge are admired and find wide support. There is no jealousy, heart-burn or anger about achievers. Achiever's position is higher and inspirational for others. Clearly the pyramidal structure is in place, natural, stable and sustainable. Historically this is established and proven. Society does need creators and knowledge seekers amongst the vast majority of those struggling for survival. Survival challenges do vary widely, but there is always a scope to rise in the ladder. This upward mobility provides hope to those in the lower rungs of the pyramid. Those at the higher rungs provide the necessary inspiration for others. Creativity and knowledge do remain the desired goal to the community as a whole.

Crisis of Overdose

Talking of maximum or minimum is quite often misleading. In fact, it is the optimum that is more relevant in the long run. Ultimately steady and consistent wins the race. Life on earth is too complex to be put in simplistic formats. No single parameter can explain the human development. Parameters change over time and with experience. For example, GDP has not remained the only measure of economic development. Environment, equity, freedom, human rights, gender equality etc are finding due weightage in the human development assessment. Side effects of every action are being recognized and assessed. Conscious attempts are made to understand the sustainability of development. In this respect, the word optimum has a much wider connotation and needs to be understood properly. In the greed for maximum we often lose the track and create problems which ultimately make all the gains illusive and even counterproductive. Similarly, minimum could be sub-critical and ineffective.

Take the case of nutrition, which is basic to human survival. Proteins, minerals, fats, vitamins etc are crucial for the body. But their intake has to be at the optimum levels. Just as undernourishment is bad, over-nourishment is also harmful. Overweight, strained digestive system, accumulation of minerals in the body, loss of sleep, mental stress etc. are real life problems faced by the people. Damage to liver or kidney, accumulation of cholesterol, formation of kidney stones, diabetes, allergies of different kinds etc. are side effects of overdose or inappropriate intake of nutrition. Even excessive consumption of water damages the digestive system. Excessive consumption of nutrients adds to the body flab. Each body has its effective levels of nutrients. Anything less is undernourishment. Anything in excess is a strain on the body, has damaging side effects and is a waste. With development and affluence, people crave to consume more and indirectly create health problems which are easily avoidable by optimum dosage of nutrients.

Twentieth century has witnessed significant increase in the life expectancy of the people. Chemical drugs and surgical techniques are playing a major role in curative health care, adding to the longevity of human being. Medicines have become a part of the modern life. Yet the medicines cannot be used indiscriminately. Dosage has to be based on proper diagnosis and condition of the individual patient. Every medicine has a potency level, an optimum level of dose to ensure desired cure. Anything less is less effective and overdose is damaging. Drugs do have side effects. Excessive intake would enhance the side effects. In fact, over-medication of the recent times has led to new ailments and new problems. Common side effects of medicines are weakness, nausea, drowsiness, loss of appetite, acidity, damage to organs etc. Preventive health care consisting of optimum medication, balanced diet, proper rest and adequate exercise form the correct approach to avoid the crisis of health.

The most glaring example of overdose is that of education. It often generates passionate debates. Heavy syllabi in schools and colleges are converting education into a highly loaded exercise in learning and a mental drag for many. It is not in harmony with the common psyche of the children, their assimilation level, overall teaching standards, available facilities, needs of the society and the overall level of motivation. This has led to many aberrations such as rote learning, high levels of failures, trauma of failures, mystification of education, professional irrelevance and overall stagnation of natural potential of the children. Education has not remained a stimulant for development of mental faculty and, in fact, for many, has become an unavoidable drudgery to go through. The overdose of syllabi has not left the education as an enjoyable endeavour. It is not preparing the children to become learners, self-made and develop overall personality. Fierce competitions and examinations for opportunities are adding to the pressure. The demotivating effects are dangerous in the long run and form a major crisis to deal with.

How much one can work if the job involved is monotonous? Work remains enjoyable if the level of motivation could be sustained. A stiff work schedule, work under pressure, work without clarity, unproductive work, uninteresting work, work without incentives or prospects etc are unworkable ideas. They will easily lead to physical and mental fatigue, distortions and inefficiency. Mental blocks are created and the mind just stops working. A good management would be conscious of these disturbing realities of human behaviour. Too many tasks at hand would leave jobs half-done or poorly done. A job well done is more rewarding than tinkering with many jobs. Too much ambition, if not controlled even after reasonable successes, would ultimately relapse into a total dejection and resignation. Anything in excess leads to a fatigue level beyond which there is only option of stress-busting change of work. One gives up the task at hand and does something totally different. Without such drastic change one cannot come back to normal level of mental health.

Much is being talked about information. Information is power, information is knowledge, it is an information age etc have become the buzzwords. This hype creation has become a fashion. What can information do without the relevant skills to use the information? Analysis of the information and its interpretation is crucial for its application. Without understanding of the core discipline, analytical skill and related capabilities, information is not knowledge and is far from being the power. Availability of information of atomic bomb is not sufficient to make atomic bomb, information on airplane in not adequate to produce airplane, having a book on mathematics cannot make one mathematician, information on swimming cannot make a good swimmer, information on a sport does not make one a good sportsman and so on. Information may be necessary, but not a sufficient requirement for knowledge or power. It can facilitate and is not an end in itself. Strength in core disciplines, ability to decipher the information and possession of complimentary resources and facilities to use the information should be the primary goal. Overdose of information would only lead to nothing but confusion and losing of the track.

Excessive freedom, excessive discipline, excessive rewards, excessive punishments, excessive aggression, excessive ambition, excessive caution, excessive affluence, excessive poverty and so on are all kind of overdosing. Most addictions, such as eating, drinking, smoking, drugging, eccentricity, arrogance etc are also akin to overdosing. It is losing the mental balance. Invariably the addictions have damaging side effects. These include ill health, loss of credibility, loss of efficiency, damage to social harmony, adverse effects on institutions and so on. The damage is proportional to the level of excess. Often it is fatal.

Any overdose, accepted willingly or otherwise, is counterproductive. Overdose is a sign of ignorance or arrogance or greed, all unsustainable by their very nature. Side effects or reaction of overdose are never selective, just as any natural disaster does not show preferential damage. Nature is egalitarian in its treatment. Crisis of overdose is man-made and is avoidable. Optimised, balanced and steadfast life is sustainable and durable. Two steps forward and one step backward leaves behind additional avoidable damages than treading only one step forward without any damage. This reality needs to be kept in mind while resorting to overdose in any activity. There are no exceptions and no unrealistic paths, only lessons to learn.

Other Side of Development

Most development studies for the post second world war period point to the rising disparity along with the economic progress. Everyone might have gained something, but those at the upper layer have gained more. The pinch of poverty is glaring when comparison is made and relative disadvantage is considered. So, in spite of progress, the common good has suffered, destitution has increased, frustration has gone up, poverty has remained intact and overall social peace has declined. Disturbed families, rising crimes, feeling of insecurity, new ailments and internal strife arising out of inequity are adding to the disappointment. Gains of growing businesses, high professional earners, double earning families etc are evaporated through variety of leakages due to wrong spending priorities and new forms of family problems. The material progress does not necessarily improve the quality of life. The loss of equity, deprivation and destitution amidst plenty, wastages of affluence, segregation on economic grounds and moral degeneration are scary offshoots of progress.

Environment is a major casualty of the technology driven development. Air and water pollution, deforestation, soil erosion, new toxic wastes, extinction of species etc. are real life problems. Global warming, damage to ozone layer, new infections and diseases are indicative of impending disasters, hitherto unknown to mankind. Local to global, environmental problems cover the whole range. These are problems of plenty glossed over by the visible materialistic achievements. Initially ignored, the environmental side-effects of development have reached a dangerous level. Beginning with pollution control, solutions to the environmental problems are being searched in an ascending seriousness. The present thinking is looking for sustainable development that rules out any development at the cost of environment. There is a clear realisation that material progress does not necessarily lead to improved quality of life. Nature cannot be ignored, climate change is real, a clear message of the modern progress.

Development goal in any country emphasises creation of employment to effect just and fair income distribution. Rise in manufacturing employment during 1950-1980 was quite substantial and helped a large section of the population to cross the poverty barrier. But the subsequent growth in the service sector employment has created a paradox of pervert income levels. While few are making big money, a large number is slogging for a pittance, although the skill levels may not differ much. Service sector jobs are linked to skills and access to global market. Naturally the global demand and global income disparities get reflected in the local income disparities. A software service provider getting salary in multiples compared to a manufacturing employee is a paradox of the present globalising economy. Salary hikes in certain category of jobs during the past four decades are only adding to the perversion and mad race towards money. It is only creating fabulous winners and bad losers. Loss of equity is not a good development. One software engineer getting multiple times income than another equally skilled engineer is strange. Few getting very large income while a large number remaining underemployed/unemployed, a few working long hours while others having no work, manufacturing suffering for the sake of glamourized services etc. are signs of the present employment paradox.

Expanding economy, industrialisation, market and organisations lead to urbanisation. It is a natural process. Agrarian to industrial to service economy is a universal trend. Urbanisation makes many of these activities economically viable. Yet the present situation, particularly in developing countries, show only urban chaos. Growth of slums, poor sanitation, water scarcity, accumulating solid waste, transportation bottlenecks, pollution, rising crimes etc. are all associated with urbanisation unless the process is properly controlled. We are still struggling with urbanisation which is megacity-centric. The prevailing urban chaos could be rectified by encouraging growth of a number of bigger towns or their clustering to viable and attractive cities. Creation of employment opportunities and attractive essential infrastructure should be the basis of this strategy. After all urbanisation is linked to economic opportunities and its optimal growth is desirable. Unviable villages and chaotic megacities are two sides of the same coin i.e. the development mess.

Development without equity and common good is nothing but degeneration. Concentration of wealth along with conspicuous consumption and simultaneous existence of abject poverty is always criticised. The situation invariably indicates preponderance of making money by any means. Cheating, corruption, exploitation, extortion etc. are some of the means for unscrupulous elements to make money. Creation of wealth with enterprise is never objected to. But skewed earning is not liked. Rising importance of money has given rise to many pervert ideas of making money. If such wealth gets social acceptance and even admiration, it would only lead to social decay over a period of time.

Services are driving the present economic growth. Many of the services are important for which people are willing to pay. Health, sanitation, education, catering, communication, transport, tourism, energy, banking, insurance, technical help, domestic help etc. are services in demand. But a fast growth is being experienced in glamorous areas such as entertainment, sports, fashions, cosmetics, advertisement etc. Glamour is ruling the human mind and there is willingness to pay for the gloss. It results in rush to earn more. This is creating a neo-rich class who are becoming the role models for the young. In the process, the core activities like habitat, health, education and transport would get undermined, not a healthy situation. It needs to be kept in mind that the strength in core sectors is the basis of sustainable community development and cannot be ignored.

Hunger may be a problem for the society, but the rich are unstoppable and appear unconcerned looking at their self-centred spending mission. The development is centred around the haves who would continue to crave for more. More glamour and attractions would be created for them in the form of gadgets, entertainment, luxury goods, exclusive vacations, grand parties and lifestyle outlets. They will continue to add to wastage and pollution of all forms. Ramp shows, media programmes, swanky cars, grand sporting events, exquisite clubs etc. are for few to make money and for large number to observe these at cost. The hungry and the have-nots will have to make good living with toxic pollution, observing glamour from a clear distance and carrying on with visual pleasures and dreams. They will continue to look at the role models and grandiose displays of the few for partial satisfaction. After all they are only the fringe beneficiaries of the development. Who cares and who has time to care for them?

Whatever may be the development, there is no guarantee that the hunger, destitution, pollution and unemployment could ever be removed. Perhaps human psyche does not accept fair play fully and openly. Exclusivity and gradation is endemic to human life. The pyramidal structure of the society is stable and there to stay. The real challenge is that of making the bottom of the pyramid palatable, liveable and humane. That is real development, free from deprivation and provider of opportunities to those willing.

Look at the Other Side

There are plenty of glamorous words to describe the ascent of human being or the fast pace of change of human life. The description in many ways is fascinating, exciting, seductive, inspiring and unique to life on earth. Man has virtually conquered the earth and claims to have achieved a dominating position. Scientific achievements and technological prowess are clearly the contributions of human being, signifying alterations in the natural habitat for own advantage. The changes are significant over a short time span in the history of earth. While patting on the back may be obvious, human being should look at the other side of the so-called achievements. There are many negative factors to this story which we should be modest enough to take into account as an introspective gesture.

We often talk of knowledge build-up over centuries as human contribution. It has also helped in improving life. Nevertheless, this expanding knowledge and technologies has led to compartmentalisation of human being in strata, seriously affecting the equity and equality. This branding and segregation of humans is rising in a subtle manner. Professions compete to find their status in the society and the winners and losers get prominently projected. Sharing of knowledge, specialisation, division of tasks etc. are inevitable in the expanding knowledge base. In the resulting competitive environment, making a choice is not only confusing but provides a fertile ground for gradation. It sets in insecurity and unique psychological problems arising out of missed opportunities. It effectively results in minionization of jobs. One gets typecast for an unwanted job and is made to live with that, a lifelong shackle in most cases. One gets stuck to undesired work and there is no escape route left.

In the present job market, services are dominating. In fact, strength of the service sector indicates the strength of the economy. Increasing variety of services is a typical feature of the modern economies. Jobs in education, finance, health, transport, catering, hotels, security, entertainment, technical services etc. are of recent origin. But for exceptions, most of these jobs are routine and monotonous. Repetitive tasks over longer duration become drudgery. That is why we find an element of frustration in all professions. Be it a driver or a teacher or a nurse or a technician or a policeman, majority is frustrated. The task is performed out of some compulsion. Given a choice, a person would prefer a change, which is not possible for a variety of reasons, particularly the bench-mark requirements or screening for entry to each profession. Specialisations, special skills, expertise and experience restricts one to narrow job options which makes mobility difficult. Any drastic change in profession is almost impossible.

Development is a primary objective that is usually ill-defined. One common observation made by experts and public figures is that economic development invariably leads to disparity. Open market economies seem to achieve higher economic growth. Yet it generally increases disparity. Controlled economies attempt to smother income disparities. But they show sluggish growth. Reconciling economic development with equity appears unnatural. Disparity seems to be endemic to human life. All development models have failed on this score. Same is the case with regards to deprivation. Progress is a gain for some at the cost of others. Yet we seek progress with the hope that the gains would percolate and eventually everybody would be benefited. Deprivation has a relative and varying content. It is linked to current capabilities, possessions of assets and the felt needs which vary with time. Overall, the level of human deprivation remains the same at different points in time. Only its benchmark shifts.

Competition is presently projected as the key for development. It is considered as important for release of individual energy, boosting individual motivation, giving impulse to creativity, adopting innovativeness and realise personal aspirations. This has been amply shown to work as seen in the prosperity of some countries. How long it will sustain is anybody's guess. Yet this freedom for individual development is not free from aberrations. Rise in crimes, disparity, exploitation, wastage, ends undermining means etc. are on the rise and regressive in the long run. Unlimited competition only creates winners and losers, psychological problems for individuals, depressions, physical ailments, unrestrained one-upmanship and pervert value judgements. A need is felt for rules of the game, legal provisions, regulatory mechanisms, policing etc. Without some social control, individual could play havoc with the societal harmony. The dangers of perversion and regression in social life are common outcomes of excessive competition.

Economic prosperity, at least the level of minimum comfort, is the main goal for most individuals. Basic needs, risk coverage and secured life are common aspirations. For a small number this restrain does not exist. Beyond the optimum, the level of prosperity could be a source of trouble. Problems of the wealthy have been understood for ages. Psychic problem arising out of lifestyle comparisons, proneness to addictions, sophisticated crimes, wasteful habits, trivialisation of nature's modesty, loss of ethical values, tensions of protecting wealth and overall isolation are the negative sides of having plenty. Just as squalor is bad, unlimited prosperity could also be bad. The optimisation is a ticklish subject, an ongoing dilemma. This dilemma is very well reflected in the mind-boggling economic growth of the last century and simultaneous rise in economic offences, armaments, military, police force, legal demands, types of diseases, man-made disasters, religious pursuits for peace of mind, need of spiritual guides etc. All these could be clubbed as the problems of plenty.

Individual cravings for projecting affluence, conflicts of one-upmanship, rising variety of disasters, rising severity of disasters, rising incidents of chaos and the situations going out of control are all creations of human progress. Essentially it is the outcome of intervention in nature. Problems of industrial pollution, transport bottlenecks, severity of accidents, work related diseases like hypertension, obesity etc. are of recent origin and are attracting much attention. Look at this side of the human life is needed and not to get carried away by the glamour of progress. Ultimately progress at least should not become a zero sum game, if not negative sum game. All are in the same boat and must keep floating. The dangers of losing the way, getting into storms, facing a tsunami, crashing into an iceberg etc are possibilities and need to be tackled. In spite of all this, human life needs to sustain in the long run in the interest of all. Making it happen is not easy and demands dispassionate efforts to look at the other side of the self-defined progress.

Contrasts Coexist

Coexistence of pro and anti, up and down, yes and know, black and white, thesis and antithesis, contradictions, opposites etc is inbuilt in nature. In fact, cyclical and balancing format of nature is a stable and sustainable structure. So we find conventions being challenged, practices being changed, anti-establishment trend existing and fashions getting replaced. Contrasts and diversity remain forever. Both sides and even multiple sides exist and legitimately claim relevance and importance. Human worth, participation and outcome, in practice, do face contrasting positions to choose from.

Choice within multiplicity remains a contentious issue needing compromises in practice. Balancing becomes inevitable. The choice may favour some options and leave out some. Choices keep changing with time. Take the case of merit. Assessing merit is not an easy task. In the competitive setting, it boils down to some formal technique driven mechanism. Such mass assessment techniques may be practically correct, but do favour some and go against some. Persons honed in techniques and prepared do better than those with raw talent. Techniques favour elitists who have means to acquire them. Same is the case with assessing efficiency, success, failure, proficiency and many other human qualities which matter. So, smartness, situation suited behaviour, polished presentation etc may carry the day, even for those who are weak in contents. This is more like camouflaging weaknesses. However, in case of technical skills, creative activities, passion in specific tasks and unique natural gifts may find smooth sailing. Special natural gifts or skills may not need much dependence on techniques to succeed. That is why we do have born singers, artists, sportsmen, mathematicians, speakers, craftsmen, innovators, reformists etc.

Any human participation faces contrast. Mass production and averaged productivity methods are technology based in which humans act like supervising robots. Efficiency is standardised with partial robotization of workers. There is little scope for personal intervention or touch. There is very little creativity at working level. Perhaps, only at designing level there is scope for creativity. Standard mass output is the result. This may be alright with many gadgets and goods. But about items like processed food, the products are monotonous and devoid of personal touch. People soon lose taste for it and shift back to home-made variety. Similar is the case with furniture, home décor, clothing, crafts etc. Shift from standardised to customised is often driven by desire for personal touch and creative instinct. Human mind is not fit for robotization, looks for new, seeks variety and tries to come out of strait-jacketing of any kind. Getting fed-up with routines and monotony is common with all.

Human diversity, originality and creativity is very well reflected in variety of creations. It may not have efficiency of a machine, but the output has personal stamp on it. Each item may not be likable, but there are options to choose from. For example, people do make choice of restaurant for a specific style of preparation, menu or dish. What is prepared by individuals is unlikely to be standardised fast food. As in slow cooking, its taste is likely to be unique, expected to have personal creative touch and possess special quality. Same is true with many consumer items like clothing, crafts and furniture. These are man-made inefficient outputs, may cost more, yet well relished and mentally satisfying. Liking for this creative mind game and choice making is inbuilt in human nature. In fact, slow cooking or relaxed working gives the best quality output. Well thought out letter may take time, but will have the best impact on both sides. Similarly, passionate art work does need patience, but the outcome is satisfying. Rigorous, slow and steady do provide quality and uniqueness.

The averaged out conventional wisdom looks into practical issues of mass application. Curriculum, exams, tests, interviews etc are for screening a large number for conventional proficiency and vocations. These structured methods are for those who are prepared or programmed for those methods. Those not programmed would fail to cross the bar. They may include, besides underprepared, those who are unconventional in thinking like creative minds, original thinking type, passionate, having special skills etc. They can't be put in formulaic structures, almost unfit for these tests. So we often find successful entrepreneurs, artists, politicians, writers, social reformers, innovators etc going through failures in conventional tests. They are admired for achievements without the conventional tests or merit. Their success is unique, unexpected and by far unconventional or antithetical. Identifying such talent is almost impossible. Their rise is beyond prediction.

Stigmatization of individual as failed one is a clear failure of the conventional structures built and sustained by those who are beneficiaries of these structures. Failed cannot be discarded or ignored. They may be unfit in the conventional sense, but need to be understood and explored for possible unique and dormant qualities. Creating opportunities and outlets for those so-called failed need to be a priority agenda for any society. In fact, this is a perpetual problem for all policy makers. Agriculture, trade, skilled services, transport, security, catering, entertainment, tourism etc are some of the important areas of opportunities for self-employment and employment which are in abundance and yet have remained unorganised and unattractive. Can these be organised, upgraded and made attractive with technologies and tools? It is a major policy challenge. The hidden talent for quality services remains untapped in the absence of adequate mobilisation efforts. Dormant qualities for simple tasks remain unused and wasted, a bigger failure for the society. Worrying only for organised jobs is not going to solve the problem of broader failures in mass mobilisation for useful work.

The opposite of everything exists. Genuine opposite is a need. It is a healthy balancing and competitive coexistence, much needed for survival. Antithesis could be original and creative. In that respect, such antithetical positions are worth looking at. Take the case of conventions or traditions which could lose relevance with time. They may need reforms. Anti-convention movements have led to such reforms in history. These are fair and creative actions, original and genuine. Gender equality and anti-discrimination reforms of all kinds are such cases in point. Anti-establishment movements in history like independence from foreign rule, toppling of dictatorships, opposite ideological positioning etc are desirable developments to meet changing aspirations of people. Taking a position against current practices on fair logic is often useful for course corrections in various activities. In a way anti anything deserves serious consideration and even acceptance.

Contrary views based on serious logic are needed for long term benefits and harmony. They are most likely to be original and creative. Emergence of such views need to be supported and even accepted as a contribution to the knowledge base and best practices. These provide a wider platform for new creations, reforms and progress. It is a passage for creative change, viable alternatives and eventual balancing. Thesis and antithesis have to co-exist. Contrasts are for crucial balancing in nature. Sustainability is the core strength of nature that compels contrast to co-exist and balance out any perturbations.

Victim of Own Success

To nurture competitiveness and merit, participation is essential. Which activity or competition to participate? It is a choice of the individual. Having joined the race, one must try to succeed. Success is not always assured. Depending on the level of competition, probability of success changes. The struggle involved varies from case to case. It could be entry level struggle, struggle to rise in the ladder, struggle in the choice of tasks, struggle in sustaining the tempo and so on. These have to be gone through. Multiple parameters influence this passage. Personal strengths, weaknesses, background, circumstances and luck factor contribute to the result. Success itself is often dicey and may play truants, unless dealt with adequate maturity. Becoming a victim of success, for varied reasons, is a common experience in the highly competitive environment. One must face it squarely.

To succeed is the objective. What means to be adopted is an individual choice. Choices are many and that makes a difference. It is a test of the character in making a choice and be prepared to face the possible consequences. Broadly, success could be hard-earned or out of luck or a manoeuvred one. If it is a hard-earned, in all likelihood, the mind must be well prepared to deal with it. In fact, the mind must have been stable enough to deal with even the possible failure. It is a sign of stead-fast character. In case of success out of luck, the mind faces a challenge of digesting it. It poses a problem of dealing with the responsibilities emanating from the success. Stability of the possibly underprepared yet learner mind is under test. The case of manoeuvred success is much different. Here, the challenge is much stiffer. The ambitious mind is burdened with the ethical thoughts, is likely to be unfit for core functions and responsibilities and may be erratic or fragile in performance. In all these cases, one's character is tested. The core strength and the circumstances would eventually decide the outcome of success and what follows from it.

In any case, the real danger is that of success going to the head. The feeling of being special is the most dangerous state of mind. Those who do not take the success with a pinch of salt may lose track and may get into a pompous or an arrogance mode. What follows is the disturbance in the externalities those, in fact, compliment the follow up on the success. These externalities include the team members, resources, customers or beneficiaries, competitors, other supportive participants and so on. In case of individual achievers, success may undermine the discipline that is needed to sustain the performance. The glamour of success may overrun the abilities which, in fact, brought the success. Successful careers ending in short time spans are common examples. There is a lesson for those wishing to sustain their careers. Don't allow the success to go to the head. Feet have to be kept firmly on ground to avoid embarrassing downfall and possible withdrawal.

Sustaining exciting results is much difficult. This is true in all fields. Academic excellence, professional achievements, business success, wins in sports, political gains, social activism etc are beset with uncertainty. Often these are short-lived wonders, for a variety of reasons. Circumstances, emergence of new competitors, losing momentum, misjudgements or shear bad-luck, slide down is a painful reality. Very few succeed in preventing such early downfall. New techniques, new knowledge, new practices and innovations emerge with time. These fresh means favour freshers or new entrants who overwhelm the established peers. In a way, keeping momentum with time is rarely possible. It is like getting outdated, preventing which needs conscious efforts to change with time and remain at the frontline. Therefore, new leadership, new talent and new ideas are encouraged to keep this tempo.

These realisations test the importance of humility and responsibility. These are indicative of willingness to change with time. This is valid for individual arenas as also for team goals or collective goals or organisational goals. Don't want to change or can't change? then quit, is the message. While humility is in making way for deserving others, responsibility is in keeping the collective goals as prime consideration. So, individuals are dropped from the team, captains are changed, some even retire, so that the team meets the current challenges. Similarly, in businesses, professional management grooms new leaders, bring in new talent, identify change makers and encourage fresh minds to deal with changing times. Even family businesses do hand over reins to next generation from within the family or bring in professionals, if need be. The goal is to sustain the good performance and prevent decline. Not an easy task, as could be seen from abundant short-lived success stories.

Caution and tenacity are essential elements to prevent from going wayward. These can deal with the negative after-effects of successes. Caution reminds that the success is not permanent and being prepared for failures is a necessity. Unknown parameters are there to stay and would continue to haunt in future. Caution helps to remain on the look-out for unknowns and possible surprises and deal with them effectively. Surprises could arise out of policy changes, disruptive innovations, international events, shifting demands, unforeseen developments etc. To remain prepared for such possibilities needs tenacity, be on the job and be alert to tackle the unknowns. Tenacity also hints at persuasiveness, hard work, mobilisation of resources, bring about changes and motivate the team. Not to give up the right path is the attitude. Chances of going wrong are kept to the minimum.

Often the problems are self-created. Calling them as circumstantial or due to someone else is an escape route that is in the interest of none. Such thought of victimhood is uncalled for and avoidable. In fact, keeping prepared for all contingencies and eventualities is a necessity, but often ignored. Not having ideas about various possibilities and not having contingency plans is a personal shortcoming. A genuine bad luck could be justified, but clear ignorance or sloppiness cannot be accepted. Downward journey from success to failure is usually a self-created situation. Unless it is clearly understood, there can be no recovery mechanism. Failures cannot be passed on to someone else and victimhood cannot be used as a shield for personal shortcomings. Foresight and preparedness are desired qualities.

Humility in success is a real strength that can remain a best shield to recover and sustain in future. It is a character that remains alert, open to new ideas, ready to learn, can mobilise resources, can motivate the team and is always ready for sacrifices. Humility raises credibility that enables summoning help from outside to overcome crisis. Humility indicates control on mind. It recognises contributions of others in the success and admits the same. Humility prevents hankering for credit and gives it wherever it is due. It is a key element to prevent downfall and keep the success story alive and kicking. It is high on confidence level, doesn't get carried away with expositions or show, keeps the balance intact and just pursues the task at hand with full strength. Humility has clearly proven its merit in all fields of activity. Then why become a victim of own success?

Toppers to Tail-enders

Accomplishing something of interest is always satisfying. Even a modest goal gives pleasure and peace of mind. Ambitious and competitive achievements do have glamour and excitement. But they are also sources of pressures and heart-burns in future life. Pursuit of such goals are associated with high uncertainties and often failures. They need single-minded devotion and dedication, without guarantee of success. There are always few toppers/rankers, few tail-enders and a large number in the category of 'also ran'. How they perform in the real life is linked to expectations and the attitudes of these categories. Their performance or underperformance are relative to the bench-marks set individually. So, the peace in the modest goals or frustrations in missing high targets or unexpected performance of the multifaceted middle order are some of the outcomes worth looking at.

Real life situations are usually complex and involve multiple functions to deal with. They are not based on singularities or one track actions. Broader principles or theoretical explanations may exist, but actions may involve objectivity in assessment, adjustments and compromises. It is the judgemental action that would eventually decide the progress or regress, success or failure. So the real test lies in gauging the situation in all angles and taking a decision. In the social, political, economic and managerial decisions, a feasible and sustainable middle path is normally looked for. One track thinking or extreme position or unrealistic stand cannot make this possible.

It is normally observed that in the well-structured functions, those who perform well, often fail in the unstructured and diverse real life situations. So a good academic or an erudite researcher may not be able to lead an institution, a management expert may not be able to lead a business, a radical ideologue may not be able to lead the reforms, a domain expert may fail in the field performance and so on. The toppers in the competitive arena of structured tests/exams, often remain underperformers in the real life challenges. Their mind-set is tuned more to the structured working than the real life dynamics. Compared to this, the case of the tail-enders is quite different. Their problem is that they are normally not tuned to structured work, not prepared for competition, not motivated enough and fail to get even the preliminary break in career. Obviously they remain under-performers in the real life situations. So, but for exceptions, for different reasons, in the real life, toppers and tail-enders find themselves in the under-performers category.

Toppers, besides intelligent, are tuned and prepared for structured functions. They are highly focused on their special skills and are likely to ignore the other elements in the real life situations. In fact, most attractive competitive fields have become brutal and need much groundwork to succeed at the entry level competition. Such narrow focus tends to keep aside the other aspects of the real life needs, such as socialisation, health, hobbies, adventures, risks etc. The structured entry tests have become more of a process of elimination than selection. They ignore other complimentary aspects of the real life performance. The consequence is that the topper may land up in an unpalatable situation of high expectations and low complimentary skills, keep under-performing and get demotivated. The pressure of rank glamour and exposure becomes too taxing to handle.

Tail-enders is basically an unorganised lot that is not tuned to structured performance. May be background, ignorance or indifference, they are not prepared enough for structured competitions. Basically they are not there in the race, seriously. They remain generally demotivated as they find the test structure unsurmountable. Extremely low probability of success makes them to consider it as a futile exercise, not worth the efforts. They are resigned to modest goals, expectations and have no regrets for that. By choice, they remain under-performers and, perhaps, do not reach their inherent potential of taking up bigger challenges.

In a way, both toppers and tail-enders end-up as under-performers. They become misfit to handle multiple parameters in the arena of real life. Compared to this, those in the broad spectrum of the middle category do better in the real life situations. They are more realistic, do not get demotivated easily, keep multiple interests alive, take care of complimentary factors, are flexible to adjust, have no baggage of rank, keep focus on broader objective and are ready to learn new things. They usually have multiple interests and the resultant mind-set is their strength to handle multiple parameters in real life. They are at ease and ready to show reasonable performance.

Extremes are positions of imbalance. Expectations and pressures on both ends are often unreasonable, unsustainable and unjustifiable. Just as miracles cannot be expected from rankers, tail-enders should not be undermined or ignored. No targets could be set based on past glory or shame. There has to be a fresh look linked to the current situation and needs. Such a realistic assessment could bring the best out of the individuals. This approach would put rankers at ease and encourage tail-enders to do better. The in-built imbalance with extremes is allowed to be reduced for better performance. In the process, while the pressure of possible stigma of under-performance is reduced from toppers, the encouragement lifts the confidence level of the tail-enders. Here, bringing the best out of the people is the objective. That is the strength of the positive management of human resources in any well-established organisation.

For better performance, an organisation needs all-rounders, go getters, versatile lot, accommodators, team players and not slotted ones or extremists. This is the middle category that performs with ease. No past baggage or hangover. They are not slotted, have multiple relevant interests, relaxed, can visualise diverse influencing factors and assess the situation better. They can do scouting, do networking, communicate well, mobilise resources, and show better performance. Such middle level achievers sustain the organisations in the long run. No flamboyance, no hiccups, no anxiety, no negativity and no irritants. They are real achievers, the core strength of the organisation.

Versatility and tenacity are key to handle diverse needs of real life. This is amply shown by core functional managements of most organisations. These are silent workers, well versed with the diverse situations and assiduously working to keep the organisation moving. They are committed, open to changes, venturing on new ideas, accept palatable risks and keep long term vision. That is the sign of maturity and versatility, typically found in lateral thinking persons. They are relaxed and at ease with no hangovers of any kind. The burden of personal expectations is kept at bay and the mind is set free to deliver the best possible in the situation. To move on is the mission. May not be conventional or standard, may be out-of-box ideas, decent outcome is the goal. Searching new fields, unconventional ventures, creative ideas, and the achievements could show new paths, inspiring others. That is the performance at its best.

Thinking – A Nature's Gift

Human being is considered as a thinking animal. The word 'Thinking' differentiates it from other animals who are known to be primarily focused on day-to-day survival. Most animals do have some special features and skills needed for survival. Legendary scientist Pavlov did study animal responses in various situations. Animal trainers do train them for certain functions, actions and uses. For example, dogs are trained for crime investigations, elephants perform in circus, parrots do pick up few words, penguins do acrobatics and so on. Yet, humans are unique and have special quality to think, innovate, communicate and progress. That is why humans are uniquely placed in the animal kingdom, a nature's gift.

Gathering information is important, but putting it together for a logical and useful conclusion is more important. This needs thinking, the capability that could be built through efforts. Developing the thinking prowess is the basic objective of education, grooming, mentoring, maturing and doing what is relevant. Aversion to thinking would only end up in irrelevant activities. It only leads to mistakes and more mistakes. Targets are missed; wastages of time, energy and resources are the results; credibility goes down; confidence sinks and one eventually gets demoralised and demotivated. This is no choice for any sensible person. Relevant and effective thinking is to be taken seriously, pursued doggedly and assimilated effectively.

Although a nature's gift, thinking has to be cultivated and nurtured like any other gift of nature, such as physical assets, skills and abilities. Honing these gifts by practicing is what everyone attempts throughout life. Any slackening in these efforts do have adverse effects. Good habits need to be cultivated and practiced. This is a common experience. However, only those committed do maintain good habits and perform better. Setting objective itself needs proper thinking. This has to be ingrained right from the childhood. This is where the family and neighbourhood inputs play a big role. Here the die is cast. If this beginning is good, one picks up the momentum, making the path smoother for bigger achievements. In fact, majority misses this early momentum for a variety of reasons and remain modest achievers.

Decision about the core objective and the way forward itself needs clean thinking ability and dogged persuasion. Negativity, cynicism, hatred, adversarial and shaky mind-set cannot cultivate this ability. For purity of thinking these pollutants have to be kept at bay. Thinking helps to understand the realities and set goals. It takes into account personal strengths, weaknesses, skills, aspirations and means at hand. It helps in creating personal image and adopting means. Purity of image demands purity of thinking. It decides the path. The actions also have to be commensurate with the core objective. One could be combative without being mischievous, efficient without being rash, strict without being harsh, honest without being irrational and so on. All these methods require purity of thinking and action.

If thinking is a burden, then only minion things are possible. Without thinking one cannot aim big or be ambitious. Only strong ability to think can create bigger picture, set bigger goals, define the path, mobilise resources and keep contingency plan ready to fall back on if need arises. That is why, people groomed for leadership and management role are trained to think holistically. They are taken through a structured training and on the job experience. Successful entrepreneurs, leaders, creative artists, innovators, reformers and gifted ones are blessed with insight and broader vision. Their persona is tuned to more of thinking, visualisation, motivation, action and persuasion to the finish.

Thinking is a serious business. Meticulous, rigorous, analytical, searching, introspective etc are essential elements of serious thinking. These are in-built qualities and also adequately nurtured to be effective. Strategic, balancing, rational, practical and forward looking thinking are situation dependent lines of action to be decided by the concerned individual. One's abilities are tested here. Decisions may go wrong. But serious thinking would include contingency plan to rectify the mistakes and come back on right track. Success and failure are taken as a part of the game and enough care is taken to keep the situation under control. Risk taking, caution, monitoring, manoeuvring and timely withdrawals are part of the process. There is no scope for sloppy short-cuts, panic reactions, regrets, weak responses, recklessness and immaturity. Being calm, composed and in control is the base level in serious thinking.

To take up a difficult task or achieve a good quality output needs serious thinking and adequate ground-work. Understanding a task at hand or the target of quality output is a starting point to plan any action. Gauging the difficulties, means available, possible options and contingency plans are important to take up difficult tasks. Similar is the requirement for good quality output. Quality is something that needs care, skill, tools and passion. Any shortcoming in these would adversely affect quality. The ground-work is needed to ensure quality at all levels of operation, the total quality management. Think adequately before you act is the message, loud and clear, for taking up any challenging task. Engineering marvels like bridges and tunnels, exploratory space missions like Moon Landing, manufacturing aircrafts, surgeries like organ transplants, social engineering like path breaking reforms etc are major tasks needing considerable thinking, ground-work and planning. Iconic and transformative developments are a result of such stupendous efforts.

Clear and quality thinking would never end up in irrelevant activities or wastage. Even a failure is a rewarding experience for the future achievements. Every task or case is different due to variations in the context and unknowns. Obviously, adequate thinking has to go into it to understand it fully. If all pros and cons are looked into, then the chances of success improve. These are relevant factors and the efforts made would never go waste. Failures are minimised and quality of output improved. Thinking also helps to adopt innovations, new ideas and new methods of working for better results. In fact, evolutionary changes over time is a cumulative build-up of knowledge which happens through successes, failures, experience and thinking. That is human creativity looking out for betterment.

Need of thinking may be graded for different tasks, but seriousness about it cannot be shirked away. Some tasks are routine and could be performed without much pressure of thinking. Above in the ladder, thinking gets more important. One has to get trained for that. All hierarchical systems keep in-built mechanism for such training. It is taken in all seriousness. Thinking ability is encouraged to be improved to meet the needs of the task at different levels. Talent, merit, skills, competence etc are terms used to indicate thinking ability and its relevance to the task to be assigned. Organised society is always in search of such a thinking lot for a variety of tasks. It is an unending search as the needs change with time, progress and situation. Struggle continues to put the right person at the right place as the unknowns are too many and unending. Only thinking ability can find the way out and sustain the onward movement. Blessed with nature's gift, humans move on.

Commercialisation of Human Senses

Satisfying the basic needs like food, water, clothing and shelter forms the core and common human activity in all communities. With development, need-based services like health, education, communication and more get added gradually. All these have a linkage with development of activities in the sectors of agriculture, industries and services. This could be termed as the socio-economics of core needs, progressive needs and the resultant vocational opportunities. Going a step further we could visualise the activities linked to human senses those include vision, smell, hearing, touch and taste. This constitutes the demand for complimentary needs such as comfort, passion, ambition, socialising, enjoyment and quality of life. Satisfying these added needs creates value. Commercial exploitation of these senses based needs, which create value, is something worth looking at.

Let us begin with the most exploited human sense, the vision. Visual satisfaction is searched in colours, shapes, sizes and shades. Considering the wide variations in individuals' interests and sources of satisfaction, commercial mind can exploit this situation. That is what we observe in the development of film industry, architecture, landscaping, art galleries, artefacts, fashions, jewellery, cosmetics, interior designing etc. These areas of human activity are linked to commercialisation of the sense of vision. It is a kind of entertainment or mental satisfaction for an individual, a higher end psychic need. People are willing to spend for visual satisfaction from a film or a painting or a fashionable dress or a nice house or a nature park or a sculpture or a structure. It is an outcome of economic progress, knowledge development, creative contributions, rising standard of living and stability. This is encouraging people to look out for something new and pleasing.

Natural products like flowers, fruits, stems and leaves give fragrance. Human being has enjoyed this for ages through the sense of smell. However, commercialisation of smell could be seen in the production of perfumes, cosmetics, soaps and recipes in the recent past. These are consumables having high value additions. These products do have significance in daily life as well as on special occasions and have influence on all. Scented soap, daily use of perfumes as at parties and ceremonies, smell of liked food items etc. are common features in our lives and people enjoy these, if affordable. This smell linked industrial sector is sizeable, growing and indicative of economic affluence.

Exploiting the sense of hearing is typical of modern times. The audio media is in full bloom in recent times. Music, songs, dramas, speeches, commentary, discourses etc have reached everyone through radio, television, electronic devices, competitions, concerts etc. Commercialisation of music and audio-visuals is in response to booming demand, commensurate with economically viable options of variety of gadgets and different forms of musical and audio presentations suitable to age, gender, region and likes. It is one of the prominent industrial success stories. Musical studios, musical systems, musical instruments, musicians, theatres, broadcasts, media outlets, auditoria and the market are all in an expanding mode.

The variety of hearing treats provided is amazing and caters to all sections of the population across the globe. Even loss of hearing also gets commercialised by way of diagnosis and use of hearing aids.

Cloths giving soft touch, soft beds and furniture, smooth flooring, soft seats, warm bathing water, soft footwear, smooth bags etc. are the examples where touch finds importance. Production of these items with touch in mind forms a significant manufacturing activity. Comfort and pleasure through touch is an important consideration in their designing and manufacturing. Extra cost is involved in giving the right touch and the consumer is ready to pay for it. A warm tub bath may give best relaxation. Soft footwear may make the morning walk enjoyable and a smooth seat may make the train or bus or car journey comfortable. Dress with soft touch, a soft chair or a soft bed are the demands of consumers. All these products would be at a price. But if the people are willing to pay, there would be many providers of these products and facilities, a good business prospect. Rough surfaces and products have their own utility and importance. Rough touch does have commercial value, perhaps less glamourous. Similarly touch of hot and cold are exploited by way of food and drinks. Uses of hot and cold water or gadgets are common for comfort and treatment. In a way, touch involves wide range of commercial activities.

The sense of taste is linked to food, a basic need to all. Naturally, taste could be termed as the oldest exploited sense. Everyone looks for taste in whatever is normally eaten. Taste, like any other sense, is not static. It could change, it could be developed and it could be lost as well. Commercialisation of the taste could be seen in the large number of recipes, wide range of processed food, variety of drinks and beverages, plenty of sweets and snacks and availability of natural products like grains, fruits, vegetables, spices etc. Food industry does take care of common taste along with nutritional value. Cooking methods, use of spices, mixing of ingredients etc. are all aimed at making the recipe enjoyable and beneficial. The science of food and nutrition have contributed a great deal to this commercial advancement.

What we have considered so far is exploitation of senses in normal conditions. If the senses are impaired, then also there are additional commercial opportunities. Manufacture of spectacles and contact lenses to deal with the impaired vision is the best example of this type. Hearing aid to ameliorate impaired hearing is another example of Commercial Avenue. Taste related indulgence gets restrictions in the form of diets or medicines like in case of diabetes or blood pressure or obesity or any other organ related problems. Of course, these commercial activities have core health angle and cannot be looked at as complementary gadgets/products, but necessities for survival.

Along with survival, and if possible, human being does like to satisfy the basic senses in a variety of ways. In fact, improvement in the quality of life is linked to fulfilment of these senses. Obviously, whatever is available for this fulfilment is attempted to be acquired. Economic development during the past century has led to enough affluence to think beyond survival and create demand to satisfy the senses. This is where industrial and commercial opportunity is created. We are witnessing growth of such prosperous industries. Anything in excess is, however, counterproductive. Any craze, excessive consumption, getting carried away, overemphasis on enjoyment etc. many times turn out to be aberrations in life. It is necessary to guard against such imbalance. Senses are precious human possessions and should be utilised judiciously. Excessive music, losing nutrition for taste, overexposure to fragrance etc are avoidable loading on our precious natural senses. These should not be degenerated out of craze. Their industrialisation to provide variety of seductive products is unavoidable. But the individual is expected to keep full control on use of such products and not allow their influence to go too far to become detrimental in the long run.

Rarity of Long Term Thinking

What vision? What long term thinking? What grand plan? What common cause? What mission? Don't bother me. I am battling to survive. I have no time to look beyond my responsibilities, my problems and my frustrations which are unending and there is no sign of relief from them during my lifetime. I have no time, energy and means or will to think of common good or broader objective. I am struggling to solve my routine problems and nothing else. This seems to be the mental status of the common person, bulk of the population. If only around 10% of those born live for over 65 years in the world, and most of them not at peace, what else could be expected. For most there is no scope to go beyond personal issues and challenges, broad vision remaining a distant second.

In a way, most persons are self-centred in the sense that they are concerned with day-to-day living and struggle for survival. They are focused on their own lives, relations, friends, careers, professions, health, faith, ambitions etc. Society and nature may be providing them means to survive, but the commitment remains stuck to personal issues, not the societal and nature issues. Personal interests, even at the cost of common good, remains uppermost in the mind. Fairness in dealings, charitable thoughts, helping hand, sacrificial actions, quality output, nature conservation etc. remain on the side-lines. Self-gain is the priority. Social behaviour is influenced by personal values and actions linked to self-aggrandisement. It is a commonly accepted thinking in the normal situations.

Most people get slotted in a narrowed scope. These are self-defined goals set in personal life. These are choices made, based on self-assessment of personal strengths and weaknesses and the situation one is in. So, goals and ambitions vary widely and persons settle with them willingly and without much regrets. That is one royal way of remaining at peace with whatever is in hand. It is a civilised, non-invasive and by far the most respectable self-centred way of life. Restrictive scope or modest goal may appear unambitious, but it is harmless and makes silent contribution to the common good, in harmony with nature. Silent workers are less visible but form the anchor for stable social order. Flamboyance and high profiling is not their cup of tea. They don't add to problems.

Generally people are indifferent, insensitive, non-committal and are just not bothered about common cause. Remaining detached is the way of life for them. Attachment, involvement, bondage, commitment are seen as unnecessary, bothersome, taxing and wasteful. Remaining to self remains an accepted policy. Don't bother me for bigger roles is the wish. Participation in common cause is not common. Participation in social issues, charity, political process and tackling distress of others are seen as alien causes not linked to personal life. Indifference in social behaviour is glaring. Not caring about others is the norm. The insensitivity is a direct outcome of self-centred focus. Even common causes find acceptance if there is a personal gain, a kind of business model. So, variety of innovative professions in the form of agents, facilitators and consultants have mushroomed out of rising needs and common causes of the society. Every service gets a character of a profession with a cost tag. Voluntarism is receding and has gone to the back seat.

Only few relish strategic thinking. They think beyond personal gains. They do think about common cause, broader issues and long term strategy. Such intellectuals are small in number and often hold differing views. Their perceptions vary, conclusions differ, strategies mismatch and consensus is rarely achieved. Intellectual debates and policy confrontations is a common scene in all societies. Policy makers and executives have to battle for a balance to achieve maximum common good. Accommodation of varied interest groups in the policy is an uphill task for the strategists. Very few are inclined, capable and willing to take this role. Such leadership roles, devoid of personal interests, are rarely witnessed in history. It is a rare combination of strategy, policy and execution with only common cause as the goal. They are rare visionaries.

There are very few knowledge seekers. Trying to understand reality, be considerate and accommodative, inclusive in approach and belief in the common good are attributes of knowledge seekers. They hold no biases, persuasive to the core and have passion to know whatever exists in nature. It is a search for truth and revealing it for common good. The knowledge build up is cumulative and unending and calls for patience and sustained efforts. There are no tangible gains to the knowledge seekers in the form of materialistic possessions such as wealth, power or fame. Possession of knowledge is a personal mission rarely undertaken. It is a long term goal very few are inclined to pursue. They are silent workers, unassuming, humble and unto themselves. They seek pleasure in the chosen work, help in creations of rare value and of long term benefit to all. Such rare contributions to knowledge and wisdom could be seen in all fields of activity which have helped in improving human life over time. Contributions to science, technology, art, literature etc has enriched human life.

Overcoming common self-centred attitude, few develop a capability to create a broader vision, accommodate diverse realities and take a unified view to proceed to achieve the goal. Nation builders, institution builders, knowledge creators and leaders of mass movements have achieved their goals by coming out of self-centric traps. Reforms, revolutionary changes, breakthroughs and discoveries are works of visionaries who could unify and integrate the related diverse efforts. Such innovative integrations have shown new paths to progress in knowledge, economic activities and various services of benefit to the people. Developments in agriculture, industries, education, health services, governance etc are all works of vision and unification at various stages. Few lead these changes.

Common cause is always spearheaded by a few. Innovations could be local, but converting them into a beneficial package for broader utilisation is a job of visionaries. Such innovative methods keep evolving, proven by few and then adopted by many common self-centred ones for benefits. So the journey of innovations from rare innovators to self-centred many is complete with wider adoption. New innovations keep coming up with passage of time. Creative few keep finding new avenues to work on, common cause being the goal.

In broad statistical terms, Normal Distribution holds good for human attitude. Very few are visionaries committed to the common cause and very few are completely indifferent. The bulk between these two extremes is neither here nor there, more concerned with self. Such self-centred lot is the normal social order, looking out for someone else to lead the way. This majority is concerned with personal struggles with common cause remaining at the periphery. Long term thinking may be lurching in the mind, but not strong enough to work on. Expecting it from them is a misnomer. Leave it to the visionaries to lead the way is the attitude. It is a reality to live with.

Sustainable Thinking

Call it needs of hierarchical functioning of an organisation or merit-based placement or rewarding the deserving or market driven activity, inequity is a part of the game. Discrimination is unavoidable. Few will rule and large section will be ruled. Only few will be very rich and large section not so rich. Only few will reach the top. So all cannot be equal, an endemic feature of a large organisation or society. Call it by any name, clear distinction between people and people cannot be avoided. Yet, making this distinction palatable and sustain the life on earth forms the primary goal of the societal action, a civilised society. Sustainable development is a current buzzword. This concept need not be restricted to economic activity. Its scope could be expanded to other aspects of human life.

We may start with the well-accepted idea of sustainable consumption. Natural resources are finite and their consumption should be such that their basic endowment is not reduced. In other words, they need to be renewed to the extent they are consumed. This is true about food production, forest produce and water consumption. Breaking this golden rule would only lead to famines, droughts, desertification, starvation and health hazards. In case of non-renewable resources, consumption has to be minimized and prioritised to last them for long. Recycling has to be maximised and wastages minimized. There can be no justification for opulent and wasteful consumption of natural resources.

Growth of any kind cannot be unlimited. It has to reach a plateau and even fall. Supply outstripping demand cannot be sustained, although supply lagging behind demand is painful. Sustainable growth in any sector is possible only through innovations and change. Except for basic needs, other demands linked to quality of life products go through life cycles and the process of creative destruction. Demand created for new useful product grows and stabilises until another superior product gets into the market. The productive capacity created during growth gets redundant and needs to be changed to a new situation. The cyclical behaviour is common to most of the human activities linked to economic growth.

Efficiency is an important indicator of economic progress. Efficiency of a machine, individual, organisation or method is sought to be improved for progress. Technological changes, training and management skills are supposed to improve efficiency. This has been amply proven during the past two centuries. Yet it is possible to visualise limit to efficiency as in case of individual's work out-put, thermal efficiency of power generation, fuel efficiency of a car etc. Fatigue, aging and physical limits are all constraints on efficiency. Only a certain level of efficiency could be sustained. Any effort to stretch beyond this limit is counterproductive. This is true for individual as well as for a machine.

Winners and achievers in any field are role models for others. But there is also a realisation that the majority would be the losers. Reaching the top and remaining there is possible only for a few. To sustain an achievement, one needs to be modest. In other words, only modest and realistic achievement could be sustained. Ambitious targets, in any field of activity, are associated with risks and are often unsustainable. It is necessary to think in terms of optimal and sustainable targets. Majority of the people understands this. Big achievers invariably become big losers. It is necessary to keep in mind that big achievement could be due to a combination of circumstances and not necessarily due to individual capacity or method adopted. If these limits are understood, introspective checks are sharpened and success is not allowed to go to head, the achievements are likely to be sustained.

Methods of working differ from person to person. Management training may show the right path, but cannot change the personality fully. Perceptions and judgements are individual traits. So, management training do not ensure success for all. By very nature, some are poor managers in personal as well as professional life. Working based on arrogance, nagging, trickery, suspicion, ignorance and whims is unsustainable. Participative, caring, motivating, transparent and cognitive method of working is sustainable. It has inner strength to sustain as it is linked to combined action and common good.

Management principles are well articulated and techniques formalised. Yet the management style is individual dependent. Naturally, philosophy of working, approach and performance of individuals vary. Ultimately this style decides the course of events. Management style banking on steady and solid performance at every step of a decentralised functioning is expected to provide sustainable results. Centralised and high profile individual management may give quick results initially, but has poor long-term sustainability.

Often, the term health is used in a broad sense to indicate core strength. Health of the nation, economy, organisation, individual etc. is the term used to suggest the holistic view of the state of the said entity. It encompasses all possible components of the entity.

It indicates aggregation of strengths of the individual components. For example, health of a nation is a combined view of the strength of the agriculture, industry, services, law & order, administration, quality of life, culture, environment etc. To sustain such health means to maintain strength of all these subsystems. Weakness in any one of them adversely affects the others. Health of an individual also has similar features. Broader view and disaggregated insight about strength is a path towards sustainability of health.

Administration deals with day-to-day working of a system. It is a process and needs a set of rules. Rules are based on certain guiding principles and are not sacrosanct. Rules are evolved and could undergo change from time to time. Yet the changes cannot be jerky. Individual fancy should not bend the rules. A working system based on solid foundation of a process is likely to sustain. It may sometimes appear slow and inert, but it would last long and ultimately give superior results. Administration is not a race for personal achievements. It is a sincere, committed and decentralised operation of a process. Personalised, centralised and noncommittal administration cannot be sustained, as it would only disturb the process.

The people govern a nation or a state. The democratic process is an ideal known method that gauge the will of the people for governance. The principles involved are participatory in nature and are accommodative of variety of views and aspirations. Common good has priority over personal interests. Acceptance of heterogeneity and right to live for all is inbuilt in the democratic governance. Such governance is sustainable as it is based on basic human values. Any other form, such as dictatorship, may suggest short cuts for progress, but that cannot be sustained in the long run as it may try to exclude some sections of the society.

At the micro level, any system is operationalized in functional entities. There is always a critical size or critical mass to these entities. A subcritical operation is unlikely to sustain or survive in the long run. This is true for any institution, service, facility or economic function. Disaggregated view of a system should keep this criticality in mind and design the operational details. Thinking in search of sustainability is core to long term survival of any human activity. Jerky, narrow and short-sighted thinking weakens the human action and is unsustainable.

Wasting Time

Time is a measure of indefinite and continuing progress of existence of nature, not knowing its beginning or end. It is an unending dimension that only moves forward. Past is history, future is mystery. In a limited sense, in our lives, time also deals with finite frames of events, processes, happenings, actions, observations etc which could be logically discerned. That is where importance of time is realised and accepted. Importance is very well articulated in the form of terms like timely, in time, about time, time immemorial, time will tell, keep time, time out, time span, speed, movement and so on. Importance is also in the very time frame that only keeps ticking forward, effectively scaling down the available time for a particular action. It puts pressure of losing time and effects on things associated with that. So we keep using the terms like time is money, time is precious, time to act, time tested, time-honoured etc. Importance of time in happenings in nature is unique and all pervading.

In practice there are very diverse timeframes. Science may talk of billions of years and history may talk of thousands of years, but humans have to deal with only tens of years and hundreds of months and thousands of days and even few hours and minutes. For individuals it is only the personal life spans, careers, professional time periods and a couple of generations to deal with. One has also to deal with shorter time frames or graphs of careers and professions. So one talks of exams, competitions, promotions, positions, outputs, achievements, awards and so on. All this exercise goes on for few decades till the retirement or the biological clock stops ticking. These time frames have a focus on activities and situations one has to deal with directly during the lifetime. These are periods of struggle, involvement, anxieties and excitements. One is conscious and in hurry to deal with the limits on time and utilization of time. All this is out of choice or compulsion as the case may be. What is finally achieved is anybody's guess.

Whatever activity one undertakes, putting the time and efforts to best use in self-interest, as also in common interest, puts light on one's capability. Putting the best foot forward, commitment, time management and making best use of the opportunity gets reflected in the outcome. Situations do play a role, but real test is that of timely actions and sincere efforts. Has one performed well in the available time frame and situation? It is specific to the individual and no one else. So making best use of the time is the right objective for everyone. Benefits could be both for personal achievements as also of common interests. So a good professional, businessman, creative individual, social reformer, politician etc would manage the time to achieve the goals. Such a person is conscious of limited time frame and needs of the set target. Time is precious and its judicious use includes taking care of personal health, family responsibility, social causes, environment, bio-diversity and many other factors of nature that sustains everything.

Importance of time in science is unique. Measures of motion, speed, events, technological functions, influence of energy, lives of species, natural resources, biological parameters, astronomical events, chemical reactions, evolutions etc are crucial in understanding nature. It could be progress of species, lifecycles, the clockwork linked to various activities and human functions, physical phenomena around, energy balance, technologies in use etc, life is influenced by time. Breathing, heartbeats, sleep and other daily routines have strong linkage with time. Science deals with time frames from fractions of a second to light years. This is a massive range having much relevance in the physical world. Our time frames are earth specific and as defined by humans. Mystery of time in cosmic sense continues and much is still to be explored. Who knows what is in store and what revelations would emerge in future. Time is simply running forward.

Literature consisting of fiction, poetry, biography, stories, travelogues, essays, subject books, videos etc mainly deal with the current times. Its relevance may remain for few generations. Largely it may get outdated and new contents may get added. Change with time is inevitable. However, certain topics remain relevant for long. Anything regarding human behaviour, health, knowledge, philosophy of life, evolution etc are long lasting as they are linked to nature and existence. Similarly history has a long term relevance. History provides lessons from the past which are valid in present. These are real happenings and not imaginations. The realities provide much substantive lessons. Historical facts deal with basic human nature and remain relevant in present as also future. Change with time is only in contents, but the broad lessons are similar, much closer to holistic vision, long lasting and nearer to core human values. Literary styles and periods in history do hint at time zones and evolutionary trends.

Wasting time is a common experience. It happens out of not knowing limits on time, misjudgements, not taking a task seriously, tendency to avoid work, not having ambition, penchant for gossips, lethargic attitude, wrong moves, lack of passion and so on. A large section is influenced by one or more of these factors and remain underperformers. So we do find individuals who do not do anything unless they are given a task. That results in wasting time. They are just unwilling to take initiative and put the best foot forward. Generating useful work is an important skill that some possess or acquire. Those who act seriously and in time do get edge and do well. For example, in professional duties, if the assigned task is over before time, one could use the remaining time to do more or help others or build up other related skills etc. Such individuals do well in their careers. Jack of all trades, persons for all seasons and all-rounders are assets to any organisation or missions. Not putting the available time to best use does not help. Even not having formal job to perform or not having special hobby or not having interest in socialization need not be the reason for remaining idle. There are plenty of other options like working for personal health, learning new pastimes, keep updating knowledge, undertaking minion looking tasks like keeping the home tidy, playing with children, taking up community work etc. Not knowing how to use time is just absurd.

All said and done, no waste is just not possible. The very fact that we are learners all the time, indicates that there are more unknowns. Our actions can never be fool proof or ideal. There is always some waste and redundancy, including that of time. Decisions going wrong, delay in understanding, new parameters emerging, clash of interests, inherent hesitancy, evolving situations etc do lead to waste. It is unavoidable. In fact, waste needs to be factored in our assessments, which includes time also. Our learning period is not waste as it contributes to our future actions, innovations and performance. Experiencing, experimenting and failing is also learning. Loss in one is a gain in another. You gain some, you lose some. As in organic cycle, any waste is recycled. Time given by one may give return to someone else. Trying the best in a given time frame is the objective for the individual. It would definitely benefit the bigger organic whole, the nature. Putting time to best use is the right policy.

Unease of Side Effects

So called progress is associated with expanding knowledge, particularly in science and technology. This essentially adds to technological prowess that raises economic activity and effects material progress. This forms the breeding ground for expansion in various other disciplines. If knowledge generation in science and technology stops, disciplines of humanities and social sciences would also stagnate. Opposite may not happen. Social sciences have little influence on growth of knowledge in science and technology. Cumulative build-up of knowledge over the past couple of centuries is so vast that no individual can assimilate even a small part of it. Obviously this has led to compartmentalization of knowledge. So we have scientists and technologists with narrow specializations. We have branches and sub-branches to focus on as a lifelong pursuit. The old idea of general medical practitioners is getting replaced by specialists now. There are no jacks of all disciplines. We have to build teams to complete modern tasks. Individual has lost glamour of being a solo performer in the modern knowledge behemoth. The glamour associated with names like Galileo, Newton, Einstein, Ramanujan etc is rare now. Omnibus performers or soloists or all-rounders are getting rarer.

Direct consequence of expanding knowledge is the expanding economy, population, urbanization, competition and ambition.

Greater interdependence, giant scales of operation, lesser standalones and stronger hierarchical setups are the outcome of the knowledge built up. This is a rising trend nobody knows where it will end up. But looking at the present scenario, we observe clearly that broadly there is minionization of jobs. The pyramid of available jobs shows expansion of minion jobs at the bottom which, given a choice, nobody would prefer to have. Driver, conservancy worker, cleaner, farm labourer, steward, attendant, watchman, bearer etc are jobs of narrow routines. These jobs are not physically and intellectually stimulating and are not liked by majority. These are taken up as a last choice. Person performing an independent and broader task involving application of mind enjoys it. Such jobs are fewer.

Expansion in services, economic development, progress in lifestyle, competition in various fields and resulting prosperity has not been entirely exciting experience. Associated are also disturbing trends which raise questions on progress. In a way, it is becoming a zero sum game. It is worth looking at many glaring side effects of expanding knowledge and associated economic progress.

Take the case of expanding services. Service sector jobs have multiplied over years with addition of new services, with different skill requirements and training. However, these services have also lead to narrow routines, long working hours, pressures of output, narrowed choices and overall subjecting one to a kind of drudgery. Doing the same thing again and again gets boring. It may be an employment for living, but physically and mentally exhausting. Data entry operator entering similar data over long working hours perpetually would feel the pains of drudgery. Driver driving a vehicle for long hours every day may feel like doing something else. Choices of stimulating/creative jobs are limited.

Development or progress is an aspiration for all. It is a collective objective. With knowledge build-up, expansion in economic activities has become possible and benefits have reached people. However, in the process, glaring side effects have also propped up. One such side effect is disparity. Difference between haves and have-nots has gone up. Exclusive jobs and opportunities have provided high returns to some while a large number is confined to a minion band. Competition and winner takes-it-all principal has increased disparity, disproportionately. Progress is also associated with deprivation. This has arisen out of narrowing opportunities for higher end jobs. Many having desired aspiration and motivation are deprived of this upward mobility.

Rising competition and disproportionately higher rewards associated with success is also driving people crazy. To win is the goal and to do so at any cost is bringing in the element of perversion of means. The rise in no-holds-barred competition has also set in the regression in basic ethical values in carrying out the task at hand. Corruption, manipulation, lying, bullying, deception etc are all on the rise with competition. Tackling these ill-effects of competition has become a major problem in keeping the society civilized.

Prosperity is naturally attractive, but do have its typical ill effects. Just as deprivation needs to be tackled, prosperity calls for caution for different reasons. Look at the psychic problems arising out of prosperity. These include in-built arrogance, status consciousness, greed, fear of being a target, personal isolation etc. Comparisons of wealth make people crazy out of jealousy. Excessive wealth has stimulated addictions of luxury goods, consumption of drugs, hatred of the commons, economic crimes and wastages of resources. Prime place for wealth, trivialization of human values, ethical loss in professional working and strong-arm tactics for exploitation/

extortion are some of the undesirable outcomes of prosperity. Prosperity and deprivation are not free from aberrations. A decent situation is perhaps the one with less of both.

The unease of progress could be partly gauged by some of the visible trends in expansion of certain activities. Take, for example, the race for armaments. In the name of security and deterrent, more and more destructive armaments are getting developed. Race is getting stronger. Within country, the law and order issues are getting more challenging as could be seen from rise in the number of policemen. Rising psychological problems with progress could be seen from the mushrooming of spiritual and cult figures, as also rising religious activities for peace of mind. Progress is also showing rise in diseases, both in terms of intensity and variety. Many of these are lifestyle related and linked to consumption patterns. In fact, some of the diseases are found to be linked to certain recent developments. For example, cancer is being linked to pollution, heart ailments to professional stress, spondylitis to sitting jobs etc. Scientific studies are supporting such inferences.

There are problems with excess of everything such as materialistic satisfaction, too many choices, luring of many kinds, peer pressures etc. Cravings have spread in all realms of human activities like food, entertainment, sports, politics, professional ambitions, positions of power and so on. Competitive environment creates liking for one-upmanship which sometimes turns ugly. Means lose sanctity and ends at all cost gets acceptance. Excesses of all kinds, put together, is an invitation to problems. In fact, severity of natural disasters is on the rise as could be seen from the cyclones, floods, viruses etc which is being explained as an outcome of excessive consumption and climate change. Similarly, man-made disasters have become more intense. In this we may include wars, accidents, riots, atrocities, terror attacks and so on. The associated severity of chaos and disruptions in human activities are on the rise. Easy means of communication and speedy mobilization of large participation are adding surprise element to chaotic events. Essentially, excess of everything is resulting in loss of control over normal peaceful life. Unease with side effects and neutralization of gains of progress is visible. Search for real causes and possible answers continues. Perhaps the situation is following a natural process "things have to worsen before they got better".

Maturity, Wisdom and Harmony with Nature

Cool headed behaviour is often appreciated. There are many well-known quotes in praise to such attributes. For example 1) Fools rush where angels dare to tread, 2) You must rush, but rush slowly, 3) Haste makes waste etc are commonly used quotes to suggest caution. In fact, wisdom is associated with a psychological state that remains steadfast in any situation. Wise consul often demands this state of mind. Not to be perturbed in adversity and not to be excited in favourable situation is what the wisdom suggests. It is also a sign of maturity developing with experience, age and exposure to right inputs. The resulting mental make-up is ready to face challenges without excitement. Maturity and wisdom have a strong bond and both grow together. Aggression seen at young age gets sober with age. Rashness in actions gets blunted over time and they become measured ones, ensuring smooth sailing. There might be overall decline in actions which, in fact, could be avoidance of unnecessary actions. Aggressive actions, many a times, are akin to moving two steps forward and one step backword. Wisdom and maturity do help in differentiating necessary from unnecessary. In a way, wisdom brings in long term efficiency, silently.

Looked in a different angle, ignorance is a common factor with all individuals. Nobody can know everything. But the level of ignorance shows the level of maturity or signify immaturity. Scope of priority varies with age. A child may be confined to eatables, toys, and close persons. School going children may find attraction for close friends, games and family functions like birthdays. Elderly school children may be more serious about studies, thinking of careers. College students are more involved in careers and friends. Young adults would have focus on working for professions and raising family. Elders are more settled in life. But in this entire chain of life experience, with age the abrasiveness in childhood leads to uncontrolled aggression of teenage to controlled aggression of youth to sober adulthood to matured oldie. Wisdom is all gain out of experience, declining aggressiveness and knowing more about the world around. Everyone passes through this chain. The difference lies in the variety of experience, attitude to learn and speed of maturing.

Crave for action is a common feature with childhood and youth, as also with the efficient, powerful and ambitious individuals. Rushing to act is in their psyche. It could be out of sincerity of purpose or desire to show off. This addiction to act may even lead to misguided action. That is no bar, as any action is considered better than no action. Adamant child insisting on something of its choice or aggressive youth sticking to a passion do not carry logic except craze. These are not well considered choices. In fact, these skewed choices often lead to misguided actions. Any amount of wise consul does not work until failure of the action is experienced by the person concerned. Time and efforts are lost and infructuous action becomes a burden that may have to be carried through the life unless one is versatile enough to come out of it unscathed. Calculated action has a better chance to succeed than action out of crave, impulsive action or sentimental action.

Fast action is seductive and addictive, but hoping it leads to fast change is far from reality. In fact, it is a misnomer. The natural process has its own inertia and speed. One may look for fast change, as time available for the person is too short. But the change is not person dependant in the long term. Changes and more changes follow in multiple directions and the net resultant is a subdued rate which is a combined effect of natural diverse actions of many. Nature has its checks and balances and no action can be monolithic for long. Diversity of nature is supreme whether one likes it or not. There is no choice of questioning it. Nature has inbuilt overpowering capacity. For example, anti-incumbency is a common feature in a democratic set up. Fast industrialization, urbanization, economic growth may run into environmental problems or social unrest. Fast changes in education or administration may face resistance. Bringing intrusive change itself is a contentious issue, if not commensurate with the natural process of change.

The element of aggressiveness is inbuilt in human nature. Proportion may vary from person to person. The graded aggressiveness is often observed in society. Simple aggression of young and those action minded is a common case that diminishes with experience and age. The category of activists is also aggressive with predetermined ideas and some kind of indoctrination. They stick to their guns and keep lobbying for their views. Activists have a narrow realm of activity and refuse to accept the counterview that exists. Another form of aggression is that of agitationists. Trade unionists are of this type. It is more like a war cry, you versus me. No middle ground. Adopting agitation is the standard method to make a point. Every demand or grievance is to be put up through agitation. The extreme category of aggression is that of terrorist. For terrorist, violence is the standard method to achieve the goal, although such extreme stand never succeeds in the long run.

The indoctrination is of a high order and even personal survival has a low priority. Aggressiveness of this dimension is a rare combination of multiple complementary factors. Rarity, such as suicide bombers, does exist.

Immaturity invariably pushes for hurry, as if targets are achievable by rushing through. Unknown hurdles are not gauged. The very existence of unknowns is not accepted and not factored out while predicting the change. Predictions going wrong is a common experience. On the other hand, wisdom and maturity brings soberness in expectations. It gives a feel of natural limits on the speed of change that could be achieved. This feel need not be leading to excessive caution. The assessment of the situation is bound to be more realistic and less sentimental. In the long run, speed is also likely to be irrelevant as the net outcome may not be exciting enough. Human anxieties, routine problems, disappointments, frustrations, dissatisfactions etc remain in perpetuity. Ultimately nothing is found to be permanently great. Excitement is always short-lived. There is a natural limit to change and achieving satisfaction. Wisdom understands this limit to human reach.

Wisdom justifies sober action, steadfast behaviour, importance of understanding realities, consideration of diverse factors and measured actions. Change for the sake of change is not accepted. Limits to human interventions in nature is kept in mind. In fact, no other living specie interferes with nature like humans. All other species live in harmony with nature. Live and let live is the natural instinct. This realization is dawning on humans as could be seen from the rising interest in biodiversity, nature conservation, nature parks, sanctuaries, climate change etc. Wisdom points at respecting nature, keeping excessive ambitions under control and try to live with nature.

Hasty actions leading to problems is not what one desires. Championing simplicity in carrying out the task at hand is what one needs to look at. Simplicity in action essentially emphasises less irritants to those participating in the task. Participation should be with pleasure and not out of compulsion. Actions of this type have a greater chance of success. Such participatory, wise, matured society and individuals would be at peace, the ultimate and desirable aim for everyone. In harmony with nature is a balancing act and a sustainable goal worth aiming at.

Education for all, a misnomer?

Percentage of population below the poverty line is generally close to the percentage of illiteracy. Prof. Galbraith has stated "There is no Literate Population that is poor and there is no Illiterate Population which is not poor". This broader statement is close to reality and acceptable. It is not clear, whether poverty leads to illiteracy or illiteracy leads to poverty. Going in details may throw up multiple interconnected factors resulting in such glaring and painful situation.

Looked at globally, literacy went up from around 10% in the year1800 to 20% in 1900, 40% in 1950, 68% in 1980, 81% in 2000, 84% in 2010 and 87% in 2022. Linkage to development level is also discernible. For example, literacy in 2022 was at over 98% in North America, 74% in South Asia and 68 % in Sub-Saharan Africa. Majority of population in countries under foreign rule remained illiterate until 20th century. On becoming independent, these countries did focus on education and speedily improved the literacy status. However, in spite of Government giving high priority, slogans, special drives and sustained inputs they are far from the target of Total Literacy with linkage to employability. In fact, as the percentage goes up the challenge becomes stiffer. The law of diminishing returns does apply.

Whom to educate and how much? The countries have expanded education system right up to a small village or isolated hamlets. Quality apart, facility is available to all. Yet a sizeable number does not make use of it. Free primary education, free books, free mid-day meal, free uniform etc. is not attractive enough to seek even the most elementary lessons. Those who wish can get education. But Education is still not a priority to a sizeable number. The reason by and large lays in the abject poverty, isolation, family compulsions, motivational environment etc. Can we educate the hungry and unwilling?

Is there a demand for education? If the literacy level is say 80%, we may reasonably say that the demand for education is 80%. Otherwise, with the existing facilities, everyone could get literate. High level of drop-out rate at school level is also indicative of lack of adequate demand for even school education. Similarly, those not going beyond school level find higher education not necessary for the chosen career. Demand for anything is generally linked to utility. Considering the prevailing living standard, education beyond a certain stage has no utility for a sizeable number.

With limited job opportunities, many jobs needing limited education, survival being the primary goal for a sizeable number, for them education is not on a priority list. The society does not have enough capacity to come to the rescue of such a large number to seek next level of education. A big section struggles to survive, somehow. What are the needs for survival? Education is not a need for many. The very fact that sizeable section of the urban population lives in slums indicates that even proper shelter is also not a priority for them. The only priority for those below the poverty line is food. Their income level is just enough for that. When survival itself is so very difficult, can they think of any other need?

Primary education is considered to be a fundamental right, is compulsory and is free. Yet the global illiteracy is 13%, and much higher in many developing countries. So, that much percentage of the population cannot be compelled to get literate. Even those who are literate will not seek any more education as it is not linked to utility for the jobs they look for. Those who seek higher education do so to improve their chances even to get those jobs which require lesser qualification. Education, in general, is not an attraction to a large section of the population, globally. Assure them a reasonable earning job and they will drop out of the race for getting educated. This is true even in the developed societies where majority of jobs do not need higher education.

Compulsion not linked to opportunity leads to disappointment and frustration. A college educated taking up a job not good enough for a school certificate holder, an engineer doing a job of a technician, a computer specialist doing a job of a computer operator, a scientist doing a job of an assistant are nothing but aberrations in the society. A large educated, skilled and trained population not getting right kind of opportunity, underemployed and effectively marginalised is a clear indication of underdevelopment or skewed development.

Work/employment opportunities is the main driving force for education in any country. If the country cannot provide this opportunity, all other requirements become infructuous. Formal education to acquire necessary skills is only of supplementary and complementary nature. Majority of jobs in any society are average service jobs, including minion ones, and labour in agriculture, forestry, animal husbandry, trade and transport. So, stakes for higher education are limited. Over and above, if even these jobs also are limited, a section of the population would remain in the critical mode of survival. For this section, only subcritical and casual opportunities exist. Education could hardly be in their mind. Education for education's sake may be valid for a very small section of the population. Most of the people would go for education if it is going to be useful in their work. So long as high level of unemployment and underemployment exists, there is bound to be illiteracy.

Universal literacy could be achieved only if the entire population could be given work to pass the barrier of survival, as seen in developed countries. Literacy without linkage to employability and employment opportunity is not possible. Literacy level in urban population is higher than in rural population primarily because job opportunities in service sector are much higher in urban areas. In rural areas there is hardly any employment, except the marginal employment in agriculture that is basically traditional agriculture needing very little input of education. By creating employment in rural areas through agro-based industries, building materials industries, horticulture, animal husbandry, dairy, fishery etc. it is possible to raise the demand for education.

If one looks at the natural process, it is quite clear that literacy level will go up only with urbanisation and creation of service sector jobs. Very small villages are unlikely to create a high demand for education. A planned optimal urbanization leading to more jobs appears to be the viable natural process for raising literacy level. Enhanced resources inputs in smaller urban centres, well spread out, may achieve a faster literacy growth. Agriculture based rural economies of 19th century to services driven urban economies of 20th century has seen a clear transition from low literacy to high literacy due to creation of new employment opportunities.

In developing countries, urbanisation is occurring around large metropolitan cities. This focused creation of jobs is depriving the large section of the population from employment opportunities. If this imbalance is not corrected by concentrating on large number of smaller towns, it would be very difficult to raise the literacy level. Unless such options are examined, the target of education for all, or total literacy, would continue to remain a misnomer. Completely wiping out illiteracy and poverty is just not possible. If we add new forms of literacy like computer/digital literacy, our problem gets still bigger. Human evolution and commensurate educational needs continues to be a work in progress.

Building Character

Aim of education is 1) not knowledge, but action or 2) not filling a bucket, but igniting fire or 3) not transmit information, but develop ability to decipher information, these are some of the expressions used by thinkers on education. All these articulations over centuries have put forward intentions about education. Similar broader intents have been assigned to other human endeavours such as democracy, research, industry, competition, finance, infrastructure, services etc. Constitutions, mission statements, policy statements etc are expressions of such intentions. Perceptions vary, understanding differs, methods change, but, overall, it is all about societal development and welfare that is aimed at.

Strangely, development is usually attempted to be linked to economic progress, prosperity. Other important elements like health, education, equality, harmony, environment, creativity, freedom etc do find passing mention and are even attempted to be quantified. The talk of human development index is one such accepted attempt. Yet no one pays much heed to it and the focus remains on prosperity which is expected to facilitate achieving other objectives. The other words those find mention are culture and character to indicate the way of life of a community. These are articulated in a variety of ways with a sense of awe, pleasure and pride. These are much subjective views and difficult to measure.

Yet, its feel is to be experienced and really felt. Essentially, character and culture are evolutionary developments and need much longer time frame to assimilate and get ingrained. These are multi-parameter societal build-up linked to lifestyle, civility, creations, human values, wisdom, visibility etc. It takes time to acquire and assimilate these societal accomplishments and treasures. There are no short-cuts or quick-fixes for character building or becoming cultured.

Broadly, character of a person or a group include a set of qualities reflected in behaviour or action. One may try to articulate character development. But it is a big challenge to define character and create consensus on methodology to achieve it. In reality, people do offer different explanations about character based on gender, economic condition, social status, religious influences, professional ethics, conventions, hierarchy and so on. Behaviour, working style, demands of the situation, responsibilities, experience, knowledge, interests, dedication, passion etc do influence the perception about character. Obviously definitions vary, targets vary and methodologies to achieve them also vary. Building character in the people, starting with children, do become a contentious issue. It becomes a job for everyone to set example for others to follow. Any dilution in this basic norm would get reflected in the character of the people. Civility, honesty, discipline, commitment to common cause etc need to be visible in the vast majority to indicate a character of the group. Consensus on methods to achieve this, though difficult, could do wonders. Yet, if freedom of choice of method can achieve the goal, no harm in giving this freedom. Different routes to good character is realistically possible and need to be encouraged. In fact, this multi-faceted approach may be effective in the long run.

Not having economic worries, basic needs being fulfilled and equality of opportunities in place are normal expectations. If there is no endemic greed, this can ensure civilised behaviour. Prosperity doesn't shift this baseline. In fact, civility has not much to do with prosperity. In other words, prosperity doesn't ensure civility. A good character desists from doing anything that it dislikes or that is not in common interests. So, a person who doesn't like to be cheated by others would never cheat others. One who doesn't like to be inconvenienced will not inconvenience others. These are civility norms, fairness towards all and so in personal interests. Rule abiding citizens do constitute a civilised society. It may not be prosperous, but is bound to be at peace and have harmony within, a core goal for anyone.

In reality, defining core values to work for face discord. This is particularly true where there is diversity. It is a breeding ground for special interests, lobbies and pressure groups. Mutual mistrust is a clear possibility. Working at cross purposes creeps in. Harmony suffers. Creating unity in diversity becomes a distant dream, denting the target of civility. These hurdles are quite difficult to cross and need highly matured leadership and participation of all to build-up understanding and trust. Such rare cases and periods in history are there as examples. However, mostly it has been discords and conflicts people have lived with. Very few communities/ countries are destined to have peaceful times. Most keep struggling and exerting for crossing multiple hurdles. In such cases, showing civilised character remains a distant dream.

Diversity, if not taken seriously for accommodative co-existence, could lead to confrontation and criminality. This forms a perennial problem for character building. Good character has no place for criminal tendency or hatred or harming others. Ill-treatment of any kind is unacceptable. Such conditions are the core of civility. Instilling such values is tried through family norms, religious preaching, liberal education, building conventions, opinion building institutions, effective public policies, good governance, effective justice system and so on. Controlling emergence of perversions and criminality is a permanent challenge. Diversity is also linked to human nature to preserve identity and also togetherness. People like to be different, competitive and free from external controls. The accommodation needed in community is also recognised. Assimilation of these two conflicting requirements build the broader character of a community. The level of this assimilation decides the character. It is an evolutionary process and takes time. Knowledge based society, logical thinking, creative atmosphere and recognition of merit can facilitate building harmony and good character. The task is indeed onerous and difficult.

More than defining and agreeing on character, the real problem is of deciding methods to achieve it. What is the way to reach the destination? There is no simple option to build character. The evolutionary process would take generations. The process passes through changing situations, new people, natural events and experiences. Plenty of unknowns and uncertainties makes it a bumpy passage. Challenges for survival, influences of unique personalities, new teachings, new discoveries, new knowledge base etc contribute to the thought process at different times. There can be no clear work plan, only work in progress with adjustments. The resultant character is anybody's guess. Sensitivity towards core human values and flexibility to accommodate others would make the job simpler.

Education system, which primarily deals with shaping children and youngsters, is the most important instrument that can help in building character. The contents of educational methods become important. Any bias in these contents would be detrimental. So everything boils down to the questions - who decides the contents? And who delivers them? Here again the character of the community plays a role. Good intentions alone cannot do the trick. Mobilising participation of all is required, a stiff challenge. So, education for building character could be a desirable theme for new focus. Cognitive science, spirituality, applied psychology, public health, environment, community responsibilities, common ethics etc are some of the topics which may provide desired inputs to create values. Professional training could be built on this core foundation. Such character may ensure common good, the ultimate objective.

About the Book

Yearning for development and progress is common with individuals as well as communities. It is a complex process, competitive in nature, knowledge driven, full of uncertainties, show interdependence, needs application of mind and demands maturity. Development processes involve multiple parameters like technology, innovation, services, training, entrepreneurship, socio-economic conditions, mature leadership, infrastructure etc. However, general contours, influencing factors and side effects of development are reasonably known. These are natural trends and the realities could be best understood with positive thinking free from burdens of biases, ideologies and strategies. Few topics covered in the book are common experiences and useful to understand the natural processes of development and the underlying human factors. The collated articles would help in taking a dispassionate and balanced view about the realities. Pooling of assets, resources, innovations and skills for development, with minimum side effects, needs positive thinking and attitudinal changes. Development is a common cause, evolutionary in nature and helps in improving the living conditions. The issues involved are puzzling, have many unknowns and change with time and situation. Handling them needs diverse skills. The articles in the book are generic, independent and each one make a specific broad point. Collectively, these independent articles try to help in better understanding of the theme of development. It covers few points of the vast theme.

About the author

Arun Sapre, Ph.D., is a Physicist and professional scientist. Aged 77, he is stationed in Mumbai, India. He is involved in facilitating research, technology generation and transfer. Well read, in wide range of subjects, he has published over 50 articles and research papers on various scientific topics. As a hobby he has been writing on topics related to human nature, social and development issues of common interests, for limited circulation. The current book is a compilation of few of the unpublished articles he has written. He has already published 2 books in this series viz. "Musings: On Human Nature" and "Musings: On Social Life". "Musings: On Development Impulse" is 3rd book in the series. He has extensively travelled and interacted with diverse academicians, scientists, administrators, professionals and entrepreneurs.

Synopsis

Survival is a primary instinct for everyone. Once that is assured, motivation for development sets in. The natural process of development involves multiple parameters including aspiration, exploration, technology, innovation, services, training, entrepreneurship, socio-economic conditions, mature leadership, infrastructure etc. It is an evolutionary process with cumulative built-up of skills, knowledge, competition, benefits and motivation for further development. It is a vast subject and is dealt with in multiple angles all over the world and has been studied and articulated very widely. The present book is a compilation of independent articles which have some linkage with the development processes.

The articles deal with specific topics within the broader theme of development. These cover only few points which came to mind sporadically, and in different circumstances. The articulation is based on personal experience and views of the author, and presented as an unbiased and realistic picture. Attempt is made to avoid projecting any ideology or strategy. Some of the influencing factors covered include impact of science and technology, competitive growth, impact of urbanisation, combined human efforts, creativity, knowledge creation, side effects of development, leadership for development, influence of social forces, individual impulses etc.

Contributing factors are many, and any attempt to analyse them and understand them should be welcomed. Such attempts do contribute in creating an insight about the underlying processes of change. They also help in giving a positive message and encourage positive thinking to go closer to the realities.

Since the intention is to make a specific point, upper limit has been kept on the size of the articles. There is no specific sequence of topics, and the articles are expected to be read independently. However, they do have broad alignment with the overall theme of "Development Impulse". The earlier Two books by the same author have dealt with broader themes of "Human Nature" and "Social Life". All the articles are autonomous, linked to common observations, are for relaxed reading and may encourage further thinking to understand the realities in the real life situations.

www.ingramcontent.com/pod-product-compliance
Lightning Source LLC
La Vergne TN
LVHW091309150826
845673LV00006B/1595